Adler, Irving  10/15/81
The stars: decoding their me
J 523.8 ADLER

SAUSALITO PUBLIC LIBRARY

JU

SAUSALITO PUBLIC LIBRARY

☆

# The Stars

Also by Irving Adler

*Fire in Your Life*
*Dust*
*Seeing the Earth from Space*
*Color in Your Life*
*Logic for Beginners*
*The Sun and Its Family*
*The Changing Tools of Science*
*Thinking Machines*
*Hot and Cold*
*How Life Began*

# THE STARS

### Decoding Their Messages

*Irving Adler*

*Revised Edition
Illustrated with photographs
and diagrams*

*Thomas Y. Crowell
New York*

Copyright © 1956 by Irving and Ruth Adler
Revised edition text © 1980 by Irving Adler
Revised edition illustrations © 1980 by Peggy Adler

All rights reserved.
Printed in the United States of America.
No part of this book may be used
or reproduced in any manner whatsoever
without written permission
except in the case of brief quotations
embodied in critical articles and reviews.
For information address
Thomas Y. Crowell,
10 East 53 Street,
New York, N. Y. 10022.
Published simultaneously in Canada
by Fitzhenry & Whiteside Limited, Toronto.

Designed by Ellen Weiss

Diagrams by Ruth Adler and Peggy Adler

LIBRARY OF CONGRESS CATALOGING IN PUBLICATION DATA

Adler, Irving.
The stars.

Bibliography: p.
Includes index.
SUMMARY: Discusses the properties and behavior of stars, including their composition, brightness, distance from the earth, motion, size, and weight.
1. Stars—Juvenile literature. [1. Stars]
I. Adler, Ruth. II. Adler, Peggy. III. Title.
QB801.7.A3 1980   523.8   77-27665
ISBN 0-690-03993-X
ISBN 0-690-03994-8 lib. bdg.

1 2 3 4 5 6 7 8 9 10

# Contents

*Preface* vii

**1** *Messages from the Stars* 1

**2** *Get Acquainted with the Stars* 9

**3** *What the Stars Are Made Of* 28

**4** *Brightness and Distance* 35

## CONTENTS

**5** *The Motion of a Star* 46

**6** *Sky Families* 62

**7** *Weighing the Stars* 79

**8** *Overlapping Yardsticks* 86

**9** *Giants and Dwarfs* 102

**10** *New Windows on the Stars* 111

**11** *The Evolution of the Stars* 128

*Glossary* 143

*Bibliography* 149

*Index* 150

# *Preface to the First Edition*

☆———————————————————
IN view of the enormous complexities of modern science, it is certainly a mark of genius to be able to write about its various phases in language that is simple enough for the school reader to follow, and yet so engrossing that even the professional scientist reads with unflagging interest. This is what Irving Adler has been doing in a series of books of which this is one.

In this book the reader is introduced very skillfully to the properties and behavior of stars. Starting with the first inquiries that enter a person's mind as he watches the stars come out one by one after the sun has set, Mr. Adler builds up a grand edifice of what the astronomers today know about their universe. By means of simple analogies drawn from everyday activities he succeeds in clarifying many complex concepts that usually have meaning only for the astronomer.

The topics covered in this book range from the names of the constellations and their significance in Greek mythology to the structure of the distant galaxies as uncovered by our largest telescopes.

With science advancing as rapidly as it is today, it would be impossible for the layman to know what is happening if it were not for books as well written as this one. To interpret the world of science to the intelligent citizen and the inquiring young mind is one of the most important tasks of the modern educator.

                        Lloyd Motz
                        Professor of Astronomy
                        Columbia University

# 1 Messages from the Stars

## ☆ THE STARS COME OUT

After the sun has set, part of its light still reaches us for a while. The particles of air high above the ground catch

The constellation Orion HALE OBSERVATORIES

the sunlight and scatter it, sending some of it down to us as the twilight glow of the sky. Then, as the twilight fades, the stars begin to come out. First, the brightest ones are seen in a pale blue sky. Then, as the sky grows darker, fainter stars appear. Finally, when the turning earth has carried us deeper into its own shadow, the deep blue sky is covered with a rash of flickering spots.

We say that the stars "come out" at night, but they were never "in" anything to come out of. They were really there in the sky all the time. But in the daytime, when the sun is out, the air scatters the sunlight, making a deep fog of daylight that covers the whole sky. The stars are there behind this fog of light, but our eyes cannot see them. We know they are there because telescopes can pierce the daylight glare and show them to us. We would be able to see them in the daytime without a telescope if the sun could be "turned off." This happens during an eclipse of the sun, when the moon passes between us and the sun and blocks out its light. When the sun is completely hidden, the daylight glare disappears, and the stars come out for a brief moment of daytime "night."

## *FROM EAST TO WEST*

Everybody knows that the sun rises in the east and sets in the west every day. Many people don't realize that stars do, too. Stars that are low in the eastern sky at sunset climb higher and higher in the sky as the hours pass. At midnight they are overhead, and then start going down toward the west. They set in the west just as the sun rises in the east again the next morning.

Stars rise and set for the same reason that the sun does. The earth is spinning like a top, turning from west to east, and that makes all the things surrounding the earth seem to move the other way. As we look out at the surrounding sky, it looks like a large hollow sphere with us inside at its center. We see only the upper half of the sphere because the lower half is hidden by the ground. As the earth turns from west to east, the whole sky sphere seems to turn from east to west. The sun, the moon, the planets, and the stars look like dots painted on the inside of this sphere. As the sphere seems to turn, it carries them all together in a daily trip around the earth.

## THE FIXED STARS

The sun, the moon, and the planets do not hold their places on the sky sphere. From day to day and from season to season, they move about, like fireflies crawling around on the surface. That is why the people who lived in Greece a few thousand years ago called them the wanderers. But the stars keep their places as though they were pasted on the sky sphere. So, for thousands of years, they have been called the fixed stars.

Because the stars seem fixed on the sky sphere, groups of stars keep their shape, and we can learn to recognize them. We call these groups of stars *constellations.* The people who lived thousands of years ago gave the constellations names to match their shapes. We still use these old names today.

## FEEBLE LIGHT

The stars are so easily hidden by the glare of scattered sunlight because they look so faint compared to the sun. The sun looks 10 thousand million times brighter than *Sirius,* the brightest star in the sky. There are millions of millions of stars, but only about five thousand of them are bright enough to be seen by the naked eye. To see others, we have to use binoculars or a telescope.

A candle flame gives out only a small amount of light. Yet if we saw a candle flame held a mile away from us, it would look like a bright star. All except about thirty of the stars would look fainter than the candle.

## *STRANGE FACTS*

Although the stars seem fixed on the sky sphere, astronomers tell us that they are really moving. They say that Sirius is moving at a speed of fourteen miles a second, and others move at hundreds of miles a second. Although nearly all the stars look fainter than a candle flame that is a mile away, astronomers tell us that many of them are really brighter than the sun. They say that the pole star *Polaris* is twenty-five hundred times as bright as the sun. Although we see the stars as only tiny pinpoints of light, astronomers tell us that they are really very big. They say that *Antares,* a bright star you can see in the southern part of the sky in the summertime, is 400 million miles wide. If a jet plane traveled this distance at a speed of a thousand miles an hour, it would take forty-six years to make the trip.

The astronomers tell us that the stars are made of gas. At the same time they say that some stars are so heavy that a thimbleful of the stuff that is in them weighs two and a half tons.

This book will tell many other interesting and startling facts about the stars. But it will also tell *how* astronomers found out about these facts, and *why* they are considered to be true.

# THEORIES

The known facts about the stars suggest many interesting questions, such as, Why do stars shine? How were stars formed? and, Why do some stars explode? To answer questions like these, astronomers have created theories supported by evidence they get by studying the sky and performing experiments in laboratories. To create a theory, scientists put together many facts, like the pieces of a jig-saw puzzle, to see if they form a pattern. Since many pieces of the puzzle are missing, scientists must use their imaginations to create the pattern, and then they try to fit all the known facts into it. This book will also describe some of the theories astronomers have constructed to explain what they see in the sky.

# A TRIP THROUGH SPACE

One way of getting information about a place that is far away is to go there and see for yourself. So let's imagine ourselves taking a trip to the stars. First we would have to get a spaceship, completely equipped, and stocked with enough food and fuel to last a very long time. We would have quite a distance to go. Astronomers tell us that, not counting the sun, the nearest star is over 25 million million miles away. When we blasted off, we would try to build up a very high speed. In order to be able to escape from the pull of the earth, our spaceship would have to travel at a speed of 25,000 miles an hour. At that speed it would take us about 115,000 years to make the trip to the nearest star. We would get a warm reception when we got there, because the temperature at the surface of this star is about 3,000 degrees Celsius or about 5,600 degrees Fahrenheit.

If the astronomers' facts are right, there is really no hope of ever taking this trip. We would not live long enough to reach a star, and even if we did, we would be burned to a crisp when we got there. No one has ever taken this kind of trip. The astronomers did not get their facts about the stars by going out into space to see for themselves.

## A MESSENGER FROM THE STARS

Although we cannot go out to visit a star, a messenger from the star does come down to visit us. That messenger is the light of the star. It travels through space at a speed of 186,000 miles a second, and can make the trip from the nearest star in about four years. After making such a long journey, the light arrives weak and exhausted. The light we get from a star is only a feeble trickle, but it carries a lot of information. We catch the starlight with telescopes, and handle it very carefully to study the messages that it carries. From these messages we learn most of the things we know about the stars. We learn what they are made of, and how far away they are. We find out how big they are, how heavy they are, and how hot they are. We measure how much light they give out, and how fast they move. We have even been able to get some idea of how stars are born and what makes them shine.

The light of a star is often accompanied by other forms of radiation such as radio waves, X rays, and ultraviolet rays. These rays also carry messages from the stars and the space between the stars. In recent years astronomers have learned how to catch these rays and read their messages, too.

## MESSAGES IN CODE

To see what kind of messages the light of a star brings us, stand outdoors on a clear night and look at the sky. The first thing you will notice is that the stars are scattered all over the sky. Starlight comes to us from many different directions. The direction from which the light of a star comes can be measured by means of instruments attached to the telescopes we use. If we take photographs of the stars, we can measure the direction on the photograph, too. The *direction* of a star is one of the messages carried by its light.

The next thing you will notice is that some stars seem brighter than others. We can measure the brightness of the stars by comparing them with each other. On a photograph, a bright star makes a bigger spot than a faint one. The *brightness* of a star is another message carried by its light.

If you examine the bright stars carefully, you will notice that they aren't all the same color. Some are red, some are yellow or orange, and others are white or blue. The *color* of a star is a third message carried by its light.

When a star looks red, it doesn't mean that it sends us only red light. It looks red because its light is *mostly* red. Actually the starlight is a mixture of colors. We can separate the colors by passing the light through a wedge-shaped piece of glass called a *prism*. The colors come through spread out side by side as in a rainbow. This spread-out arrangement of the colors in light is called a *spectrum*. The rainbow is the spectrum of the sun, made when raindrops, acting like prisms, separate the colors of sunlight and spread them out. Sometimes you can see this spectrum on your bathroom wall when sunlight is reflected from the beveled edge of your mirror. The edge of the mirror is wedge-shaped, so it acts like a prism and separates the colors. Astronomers make photographs of the spectra of many stars they study. The spectrum is a fourth message carried by the light of a star.

Starlight brings us four messages: direction, brightness, color, and the spectrum. These messages are in code. Now we shall see how the astronomers cracked this code, so that they could understand what the messages say.

# 2 Get Acquainted with the Stars

## ☆ THE TURNING SKY SPHERE

The stars look like bright spots painted on the sky sphere. We are at the center of this imaginary sphere, and we see it from the inside. As the earth spins from west to east, the

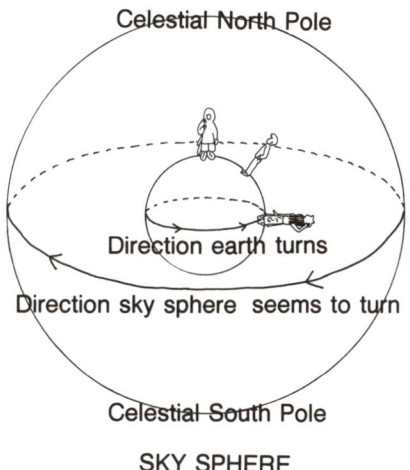

SKY SPHERE

sky sphere seems to turn the other way. It turns around the same axis as the earth. Every point on the sky sphere travels around in a circle, except the two points that are on the axis. The one above the North Pole of the earth is called the celestial north pole, or north pole of the sky. The other one is called the celestial south pole. On the previous page, three people are shown standing on the earth. One is at the North Pole; one is at the equator; and the other is standing between the two. The turning sky looks different to each of them. The person standing at the North Pole sees the north pole of the sky right over his head. As the sky sphere turns, every star he sees makes a complete circle but stays

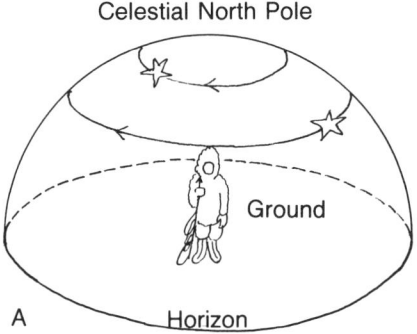

at the same height all the time. The higher stars make smaller circles, the lower stars make bigger ones. This is shown in diagram *A*. The way he sees them, no star rises or sets. Those stars that are above the horizon stay above all the time. Those that are below the horizon are hidden by the ground all the time, so he never sees them.

The person standing at the equator is facing east. You can see what the turning sky looks like to him by holding the drawing so that his figure is upright. He will see the north pole of the sky on the horizon at his left, and the south pole of the sky at his right. All stars will rise in the east, follow an arch across the sky, and then set in the west. He will have a chance to see every star that is bright enough to be seen, because half of the circle it follows is above the horizon. All the circles are standing straight up as shown in Diagram *B*.

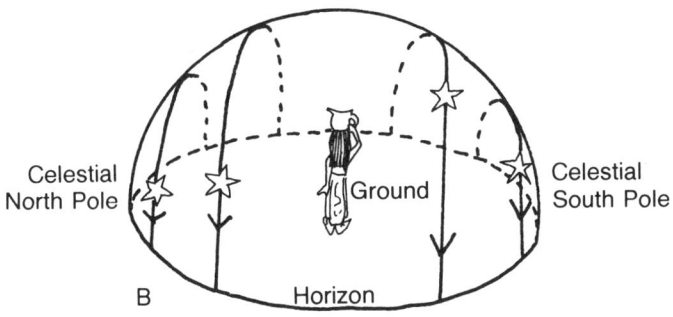

The person standing between the North Pole and the equator gets a different kind of view. If he faces north, he will see the north pole of the sky above the horizon, as shown in Diagram *C*. The farther he is from the equator, the higher he will see the north pole of the sky. Stars that are close to the north pole of the sky will travel around the pole in small circles that are always above the horizon. So these stars will never set. Stars that are close to the south pole of the sky will follow small circles that are always hidden by the ground. These stars will never rise, so he won't get a chance to see them at all. The stars that are in between these extreme positions will follow larger circles that are only partly hidden by the ground. These stars will rise in the east and set in the west. If you live in the United States or Canada, this is what the turning sky will look like to you.

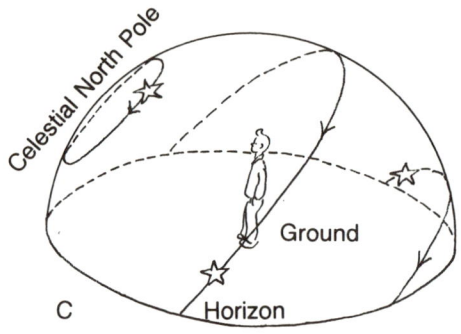

## THE CHANGING SKY

If you watch the stars that rise and set, you will notice that every day they rise a little earlier, and so will set earlier, too. A star that rises in the east at 6 P.M. today will be overhead at midnight, and will set at 6 A.M. tomorrow morning. One month from now it will rise at 4 P.M., while the sun is still out. At 6 P.M. it will have climbed one third of the way up the sky. It will be overhead at 10 P.M. At midnight it will be on its way down toward the west, and it will set at 4 A.M. Every month the star will rise and set two hours earlier. Two months from now it will rise at 2 P.M. and set at 2 A.M. Three months from now it will rise at noon and set at midnight. Six months from now it will rise at 6 A.M. and set at 6 P.M. But then it will be out only in the daytime, so we won't see it at night at all. Because the stars rise and set earlier month by month, the whole sky shifts with the seasons. Stars that you see in the east in the evening at springtime will be overhead on a summer evening. In the fall you will find them in the west just after sunset, themselves about to set. In the wintertime you won't see them at night at all, because they will have already set. That's why there are winter stars and summer stars, spring stars and fall stars. When we look for stars in the sky, we have to know the season when we can find them out at night.

The stars shift with the seasons because of the motion of the earth around the sun. In diagram *D* you see the sun at the center of the sky sphere. The earth makes a trip around the sun once a year. On the right we see the earth's position in the wintertime. Six months later, in the summertime, it is on the other side of the sun. As the earth spins on its axis, it is daytime for us when our part of the

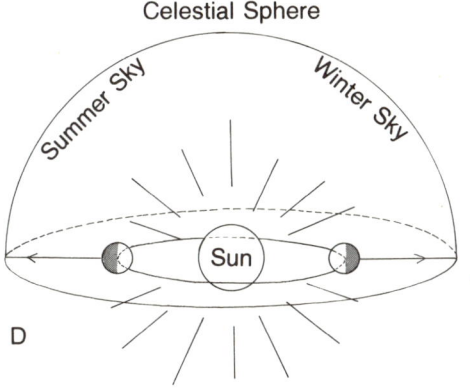

earth faces toward the sun. It is nighttime for us when our part of the earth faces away from the sun. The arrow on the right shows the direction in which we are looking when we face away from the sun to look at the stars overhead at midnight in the wintertime. The stars that we see then are the stars that are in that part of the sky sphere. Six months later, when the earth is on the other side of the sun, the midnight sky is in the opposite direction, and so we see a different group of stars in the summertime.

## STARS THAT NEVER SET

If you live in the United States or Canada, the easiest constellations for you to learn are those that are near the

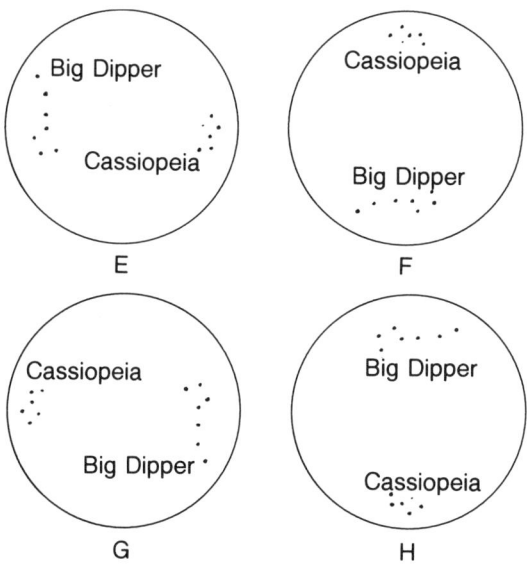

north pole of the sky. They travel in small circles around the pole and never set, so you can see them any night of the year. If you face north on August first at about 10 P.M., you will find the *Big Dipper* and *Cassiopeia* in the positions shown in diagram *E*. Diagram *F* shows how they look at 10 P.M. on November first. Diagram *G* is for 10 P.M. on

February first. And diagram *H* is for 10 P.M. on May first. Notice that Cassiopeia looks like a big W.

The two stars in the bowl of the Big Dipper that are farthest from its handle are named *Merak* and *Dubhe.* They are known as the *pointers* because a line from Merak through Dubhe points to Polaris, which is about halfway between the Big Dipper and Cassiopeia. Polaris is very close to the north pole of the sky. Because it moves very little as the sky turns, you can always find it in about the same place in the sky. In the days before the compass was invented, sailors let Polaris guide them on their voyages. They knew that when they faced Polaris they were facing north.

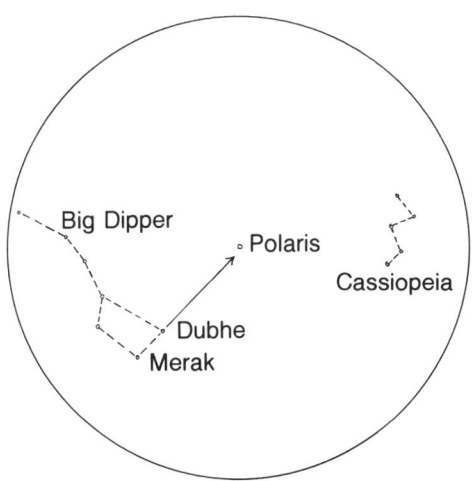

## *POURING FROM DIPPER TO DIPPER*

Polaris is at the end of the handle of the *Little Dipper.* In the evening on August first, the Little Dipper curves up and to the west away from Polaris. At midnight its bowl would be upside down, and the Big Dipper would be under it. If we imagine the Little Dipper filled with water, the water would spill from the Little Dipper into the Big Dipper. Twelve hours later, the Big Dipper would be upside down above Polaris, and the water would pour back again into the Little Dipper below.

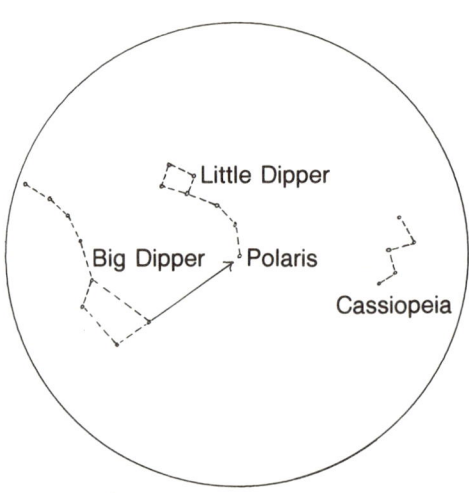

## THE DRAGON

Starting between the two dippers, a chain of stars curves around the bowl of the Little Dipper and then curves upward, ending in a four-sided figure that is nearly overhead in the summertime. This is *Draco,* the dragon that the Roman legend says Minerva hurled into the sky. The four-sided figure is its head.

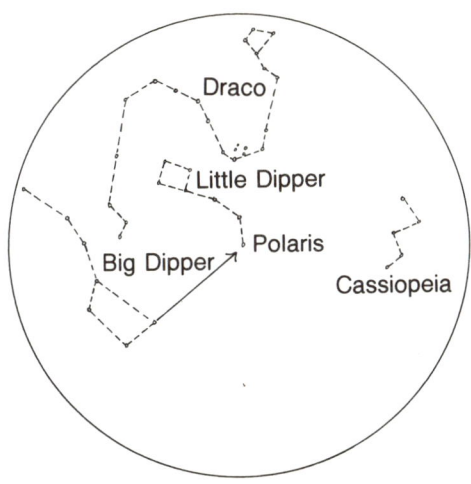

## THE ROYAL FAMILY

The constellation Cassiopeia was given its name by the ancient Greeks thousands of years ago. They connected it with a legend they told about the royal family of Ethiopia. Cassiopeia was the wife of Cepheus, king of Ethiopia. They had a daughter named Andromeda. Cassiopeia offended the sea nymphs by saying that she was more beautiful than they were. To punish her, Neptune, god of the sea, sent a sea monster to attack the coast of Ethiopia. He also ordered that the Princess Andromeda should be given to the monster as a sacrifice. Andromeda was chained to a rock on the shore, but she was rescued by Perseus, who killed the monster. All the characters in this exciting story were later placed in the sky, so each one is now a constellation.

*Cepheus* lies between Cassiopeia and Draco. You can recognize Cepheus as a square with a triangle attached. With her husband Cepheus on one side of her, Cassiopeia has her daughter *Andromeda* on the other. You can recognize Andromeda as the line of four bright stars leading up to the great square of *Pegasus*. Near the middle of this line of stars, and lying on the same side as Cassiopeia, is a faint patch of light known as the *Great Nebula in Andromeda*. To see it best with the naked eye, don't look directly at it —look at it out of the corner of your eye.

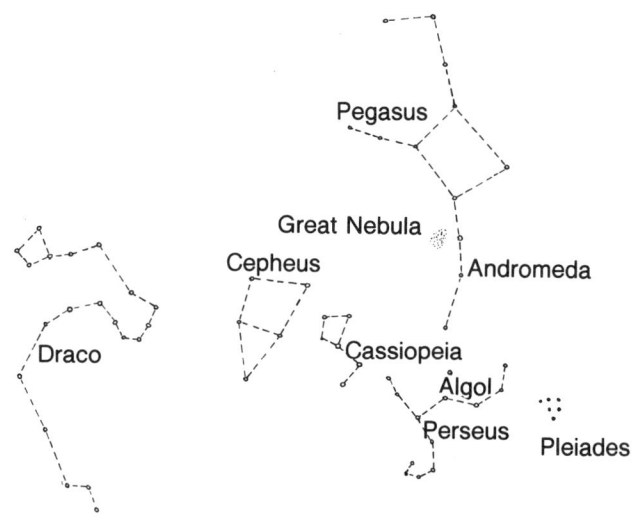

FACING NORTH

When Cassiopeia is high in the sky, you can see *Perseus*, a curved chain of stars stretching from Cassiopeia toward a little group of six stars crowded together. This group of six stars, shaped like a tiny dipper, is known as the *Pleiades*.

## GREEK-LETTER NAMES

Many stars have names of their own that they were given a long time ago. In addition, astronomers find it convenient to give them another name that shows what constellation they belong to. Each bright star is tagged with a letter of the Greek alphabet, and then the letter, combined with the name of the constellation, serves as a name for the star. The following diagram shows the stars α (alpha), β (beta), γ (gamma), δ (delta), and ι (iota) in the constellation Cepheus. *Delta-Cephei* is especially interesting because its brightness is not steady. It grows brighter and dimmer with a regular rhythm about every five and a half days.

Another star that changes in brightness can be seen in the constellation Perseus, between the curved chain of stars and Andromeda. It grows brighter and dimmer about

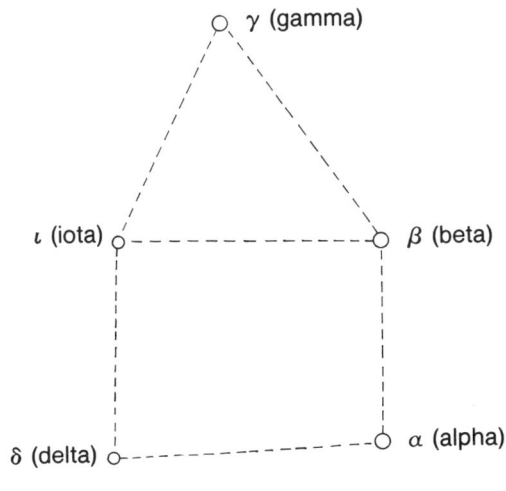

CEPHEUS

every three days. Hundreds of years ago the Arabs noticed it blinking that way and gave it the name *Algol* (the Demon). The best time to look for Algol is in the fall, when it is high in the sky.

## THE MILKY WAY

In big cities the dust in the air and the glow of the city lights hide the fainter stars, so only the brighter stars can be seen. Out in the country, where dust and stray light do not interfere, you can see many more stars, and you can see the *Milky Way*. The Milky Way is an irregular band of light that stretches across the sky forming an almost perfect circle on the sky sphere. At midnight on August first it is high in the sky, running from north to south. The Milky Way is made up of thousands of millions of stars. Most of them are too faint to be seen as separate stars, but their light is combined to make the glow of the Milky Way. Cassiopeia and Perseus lie in the Milky Way. Cepheus is partly in the Milky Way.

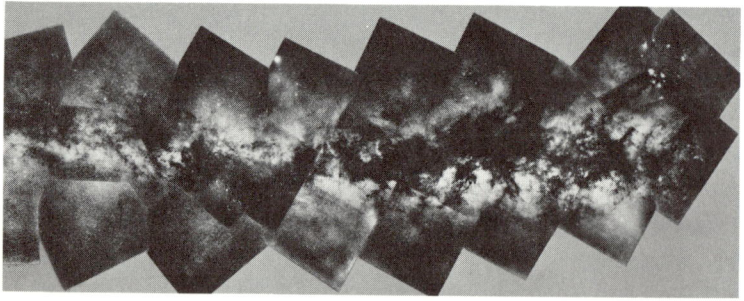

Photographs of small sections of the summer sky were put together to make this picture of the Milky Way. The bright patches shine with the combined light of thousands of stars. The dark patches in the center are dust clouds that block the light of the stars behind them. YERKES OBSERVATORY

## OTHER SUMMER STARS

Look at the four stars that form the head of Draco. The brightest of the four is called *Etamin*. A line drawn through Etamin from the star in the opposite corner of the head leads to the very bright star *Vega*, in the constellation *Lyra*. You will find Lyra almost directly over your head on summer evenings.

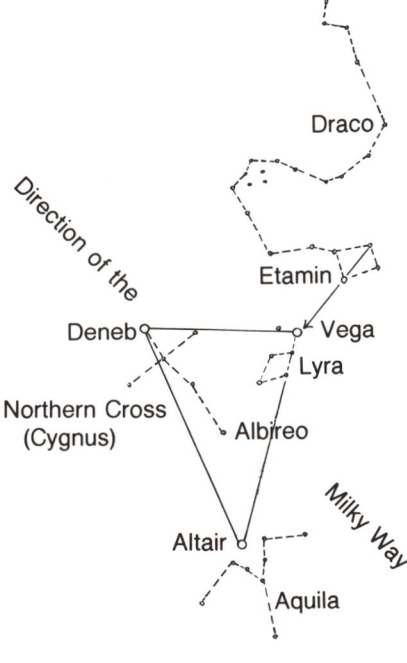

FACING SOUTH

If you continue the line from Etamin through Vega, it leads to the *Northern Cross*. The Northern Cross is part of the constellation *Cygnus* (the Swan), and lies in the Milky

Way. The long line of the cross shows the direction that the Milky Way band takes across the sky. The top of the cross is its brightest star. It is called *Deneb,* an Arabic word meaning "tail," because it represented the tail of the swan. The bottom of the cross is called *Albireo.* The Milky Way leads from the Northern Cross southward to *Aquila* (the Eagle), whose brightest star is *Altair.* The three very bright stars—Vega, Deneb, and Altair—form a big triangle that can easily be seen high in the summer sky. It is known as the summer triangle.

When the Big Dipper is high in the sky, it can help you locate the bright orange star *Arcturus,* in the constellation *Boötes* (the Ploughman). Follow the curve of the handle of the Dipper away from the bowl, and it leads you to Arcturus. Boötes is shaped like a kite, and Arcturus is the tip of the bottom of the kite.

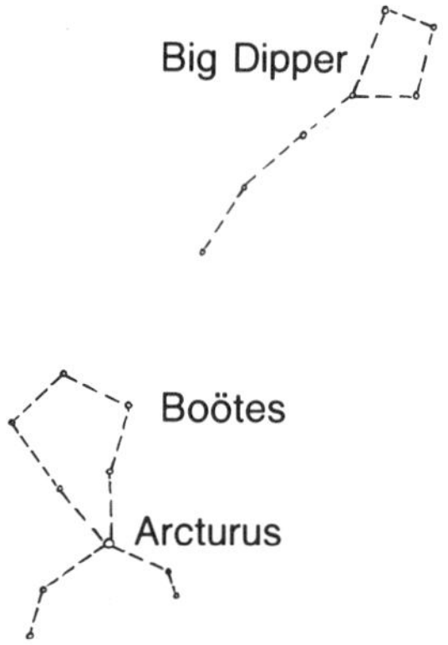

Big Dipper

Boötes
Arcturus

Another summer constellation that is easy to recognize is *Scorpius* (the Scorpion). You will find it low in the southern part of the sky in the Milky Way. It is shaped like a fishhook. The brightest star in it is distinctly red in color, the bright star *Procyon* in the constellation *Canis Minoris* (the Small Dog). Sirius, Procyon, and Betelgeuse form a triangle with equal sides.

Between Orion and Polaris is a large five-sided figure in the Milky Way. This is the constellation *Auriga.* Its brightest star is *Capella* (the Goat). Three faint stars near Capella are known as the *Kids.*

## *MEASURING DIRECTION*

The direction of a star is pointed out by a line that runs from us to the star. The light of the star comes to us from that direction. The "position" of the star on the imaginary sky sphere is the place where this direction line crosses the sphere. When one star seems near another on the sky sphere, it does not mean that the stars are really close to each other. It means only that we see them in almost the same direction. In the following diagram, *a, b, c,* and *d* represent four stars in space. The sky sphere is drawn as though it were farther away from us than any of the stars.

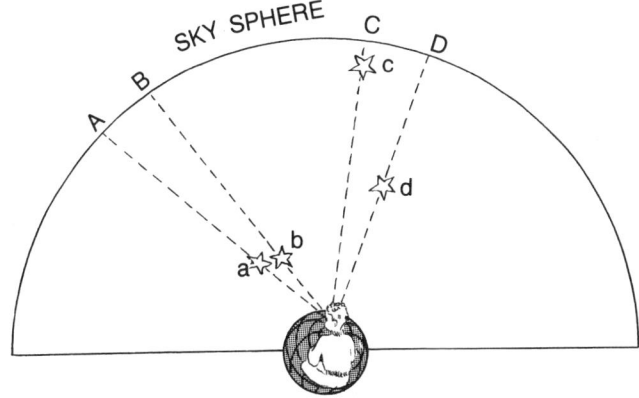

When we look at these stars, star *a* seems to be at point *A* on the sky sphere; star *b* is seen at point *B*; star *c* is seen at point *C*; and star *d* is seen at point *D*. Notice that stars *a* and *b* are close to each other, and seem close on the sky sphere, at *A* and *B*. Stars *c* and *d* are not close to each other, but they also seem close on the sky sphere, at *C* and *D*. They seem close because they lie in almost the same direction.

We measure differences in direction by the amount of turning needed to turn from one direction to another. The amount of turning is called the *angle* between the two directions, and is measured in *degrees*. When the minute

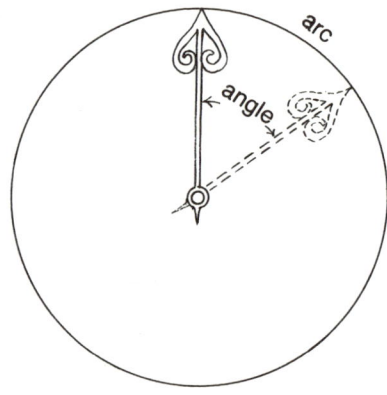

hand of a clock makes a complete trip around the face of the clock, it turns through 360 degrees. While the hand of a clock turns, the tip of the hand travels around in a circle. The angle through which the hand turns is matched by the part of the circle over which the tip of the hand travels. A part of a circle is called an *arc*. When the hand turns one degree, we call the arc that the tip of the hand travels over one degree of arc. So when the hand travels more than one degree, for every degree in the angle there will be one degree of arc in the arc that matches it. The number of degrees in an angle is the same as the number of degrees in the arc that belongs to the angle.

To measure the difference in direction from one star to another, we turn the direction line of one star until it reaches the direction line of the other. As the direction line turns, the point where it crosses the sky sphere moves along a circle, just as the tip of a minute hand does. So the angle between the two directions is matched by an arc of the same number of degrees on the sky sphere. When two stars are 5 degrees apart on the sky sphere, it means that their direction lines form an angle of 5 degrees. In the Big Dipper, the pointer stars Merak and Dubhe are about 5 degrees apart. Etamin (in Draco) and Vega (in Lyra) are about 12 degrees apart.

Since there are 360 degrees in a circle, 1 degree is a rather small arc. If a penny is held up against the sky forty-three inches from your eye, its image on the sky sphere is 1 degree wide. But small as it is, it is quite big compared to many arcs we have to measure in the sky. The width of the sun and the moon as we see them in the sky is only about half a degree. To measure arcs that are less than a degree, we divide a degree into sixty equal parts called *minutes*. And to measure arcs that are less than a minute, we divide a minute into sixty equal parts called *seconds*.

# 3 What the Stars Are Made Of

## ☆ WHO TOUCHED THE LETTER?

Suppose you receive a letter from a distant city. Could you find out which people touched the letter before it was sealed? You could, if you examined the fingerprints on the letter. Fingerprints are made up of many lines. The lines are different for different people. So if you compare the fingerprints on the letter with the fingerprints of your friends in the distant city, you could find out which of them touched the letter.

Astronomers use the same idea to find out what chemical elements there are on the surface of a star. The light from a star is like a letter that it sends us. Every chemical element on the surface of the star puts its fingerprint on the light before it leaves the star. By comparing the fingerprints on the starlight with the fingerprints of all the elements we know, we find out which ones are on the surface of the star.

## THE FINGERPRINTS OF THE ELEMENTS

The fingerprints of the elements on a star are found in the spectrum of the star. The spectrum is formed by separating the colors in a narrow beam of light from the star and arranging them side by side as in a rainbow. When this is done, astronomers find that the bright band of colors in the spectrum is striped with a series of dark lines. Each line is a color that is faint in the spectrum. It looks dark against the background of the brighter colors that surround it. The lines help us identify the chemical elements on the star because each element is responsible for putting definite lines in the spectrum.

## COLOR SIGNALS FROM THE ATOM

The dark lines in the spectrum are like identification tags for the elements because of the special connection between light and atoms. Light is a signal from the atom. When a solid or a liquid is made hot enough, it begins to glow. The glow is made up of light sent out by the atoms and molecules in the solid or liquid. When a spectrum is made by separating the colors of this light, it is a continuous spectrum, with no breaks or stripes in it. No colors are missing from this kind of spectrum.

A gas, too, can be made to glow by heating it, or by passing an electric spark through it. If the gas is dense, so that the atoms in it are crowded together, it also has a continuous spectrum showing all colors. But if the gas is spread out thin, so that the atoms are not so crowded, then it glows in a different way. Then, instead of sending out all colors, the atoms send out only certain special colors, and the spectrum is a series of bright stripes separated by blank spaces. Each chemical element has its own special set of colors that it sends out, and it can be recognized by these colors. For example, when sodium atoms glow, they send out yellow light. You can see this sodium yellow by sprinkling some ordinary table salt over a gas flame. Sodium is one of the elements in the salt. The heat of the flame separates some of the sodium atoms from the salt and makes them glow. The yellow glow is like a message from the sodium atoms saying, "Here we are." When neon atoms glow, they send out red light. This is the red you see in the neon signs that many stores use.

## *VIBRATIONS IN SPACE*

Light is an electric and magnetic vibration that travels through space. A vibration is a movement that is repeated over and over again. In light the vibrations are repeated so fast that there are thousands of millions of them in a second. The number of vibrations that there are in a second is called the *frequency* of the light. Physicists have shown that every color has its own frequency. In fact, colors are different because their frequencies are different. The frequency of green light is 600 million million vibrations per second. Violet light vibrates faster than this, and red light vibrates slower. Besides the vibrations that we see as colors, there are other vibrations of the same kind that we cannot see. Vibrations that have a higher frequency than violet are called *ultraviolet.* We can't see them with our eyes, but we can detect them with photographic plates. Light vibrations that have a lower frequency than red are called *infrared.* We can't see them with our eyes, but we can detect them with heat-measuring instruments. Radio stations send out vibrations of the same kind as light, but with a much lower frequency than the infrared. The stations you receive on your radio have frequencies between half a million and one and a half million vibrations per second.

## THE WAVELENGTHS OF LIGHT

While light is vibrating it is also traveling through space at a speed of 186,000 miles a second. The distance that a color travels during the short time that it takes to make one vibration is called its *wavelength.* Among the colors that we can see, violet has the highest frequency. Because it makes a large number of vibrations in a second, each vibration takes only a short period of time. In that short time the light will travel only a short distance, so violet light has a short wavelength. Red light has the lowest frequency of all the colors we can see. Because it makes fewer vibrations in a second than violet does, each vibration takes a longer period of time. In that longer time it travels a greater distance. So red light has a longer wavelength than violet light.

The wavelengths of light are very small, so a tiny unit called the *angstrom* is used to measure them. The angstrom is so small that 10,000,000 angstroms is about one quarter of an inch. The wavelength of violet light is about 4,000 angstroms. The wavelength of red light is about 8,000 angstroms.

When physicists study the colors sent out by glowing atoms, they measure the wavelengths of these colors. The yellow light of sodium is made up of two slightly different colors whose wavelengths are 5,890 angstroms and 5,896 angstroms. Calcium sends out two violet colors whose wavelengths are 3,968 angstroms and 3,933 angstroms. Hydrogen sends out red light whose wavelength is 6,563 angstroms, blue light whose wavelength is 4,861 angstroms, and other colors with shorter wavelengths as well.

## *REVERSING THE SIGNAL*

When atoms glow, they are like little radio stations, each one sending out its own program. But an atom can also be a receiver. When light passes it by, it picks up some of that light, soaking it up the way a sponge soaks up water. And just as a radio receiver picks up only the station to which it is tuned, an atom picks up only the colors to which it is tuned. It picks up only those colors that it sends out when it glows. In laboratory experiments, if light of all colors coming from a hot source is passed through a cooler gas, the atoms in the gas remove from the light the special colors to which they are tuned. Sodium removes some of the yellow light whose wavelengths are 5,890 angstroms and 5,896 angstroms. Calcium removes some of the violet light whose wavelengths are 3,968 angstroms and 3,933 angstroms. Hydrogen removes red light with wavelength 6,563 angstroms, blue light with wavelength 4,861 angstroms, and some other colors with smaller wavelengths. Then when the colors that remain in the light are separated to form a spectrum, the colors that were removed by the atoms show up as dark lines in the spectrum.

So there are two ways of identifying atoms by means of light. We can recognize them by the color signals they send out. We can also recognize them when they reverse the signal and remove these colors from mixed light that passes them.

## THE STUFF OF THE STARS

The spectrum of a star is a continuous spectrum crossed by dark lines. This shows us first that the inside of a star is hot enough to glow with all colors. But the dark lines tell us that when the light leaves the star, some of the colors are partly removed. So there must be a cooler layer of gas at the surface that the light passes through. Because this layer is responsible for the reversed dark-line signals of the atoms, it is known as the reversing layer. By studying the dark lines in the spectrum, astronomers have found that *the chemical elements in the stars and in the sun are all elements that are found on the earth.*

The fact that the elements in the sun and in the stars are all found on the earth was not proved all at once. It was slow, painstaking work. The dark lines showed colors that were removed by the atoms in the reversing layer. It was necessary to compare these colors with the colors given out by glowing atoms in the laboratory. You can see how big a job this was from the fact that there are over ten thousand lines in the spectrum of the sun. But the job was done.

## THE DISCOVERY OF HELIUM

The sunlight we usually see is light that comes from the hot interior of the sun and passes through the cooler reversing layer at the surface before it reaches us. So its spectrum is a continuous band of colors crossed by dark lines. But sometimes we can see sunlight that comes from the reversing layer itself. This happens during an eclipse of the sun, when the moon blocks off the main part of the sun's light. Then the light that comes from the reversing layer can be seen as a brief flash from the sun's atmosphere just before it, too, is completely hidden by the moon. In this flash, the atoms of the reversing layer reveal themselves by the light they send out rather than by the light they soak up. When the colors in this flash are separated as a spectrum, they form a series of bright lines that match the dark lines in the dark-line spectrum. In the year 1868, lines were found in this flash spectrum that did not

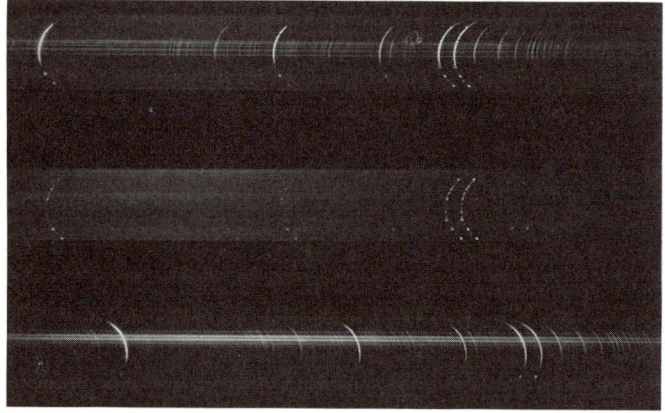

Flash spectrum of the sun, taken at the total eclipse of January 24, 1925. The element helium was discovered in the year 1868 when its "fingerprints" were found among the lines in a spectrum like this one. HALE OBSERVATORIES

belong to any element known on earth. So scientists named the element that caused these lines *helium,* or the sun element. The discovery of helium in the sun seemed to show that there are chemical elements in the sun and stars that are not found on the earth. But in 1895 it was proved that helium does exist on the earth, right in the air. Then, in 1917, gas wells were found containing large quantities of helium.

# 4 Brightness and Distance

## ☆ THE SCALE OF BRIGHTNESS

One of the coded messages we get from a star is the brightness with which it shines in the sky. There is a lot of information hidden in this message. To get at the information it is first necessary to measure the brightness of the star. The brightness of a star is measured on a special scale, the scale of *star magnitudes.* On this scale high numbers are used for very faint stars, and low numbers are used for very bright stars. The brighter a star is, the lower its magnitude is. The faintest stars we can see with the naked eye are stars of the sixth magnitude. Stars that are 2½ times as bright as sixth magnitude are called fifth-magnitude stars. Stars that are 2½ times as bright as fifth-magnitude are called fourth-magnitude stars, and so on. Whenever the brightness of two stars differs by one magnitude, it means that the brighter one is 2½ times as bright as the fainter one. If a star is less than 2½ times as bright as another, then their magnitudes differ by less than 1. So, in measuring the brightness of a star in magnitudes, fractions as well as whole numbers have to be used.

A star that is almost exactly first magnitude is Aldebaran, in the constellation Taurus. But Aldebaran is not the brightest star in the sky. To measure the brighter stars, we have to use numbers lower than 1. The brightness that is one magnitude below first magnitude is called zero magnitude. The brightness that is one magnitude below zero magnitude is called $-1$ (minus one) magnitude. If there were a star one magnitude brighter than that, it would have $-2$ (minus two) magnitude. But no star is actually that bright in the sky. The brightest star, Sirius, has magnitude $-1.58$. The sun, the brightest object in the sky, has magnitude $-26.72$.

You can learn how to estimate the magnitudes of stars by comparing them with several typical stars. Vega, in the constellation Lyra, is almost zero magnitude. Not far from Vega is the head of Draco, made up of four stars of differing brightness. Etamin, the brightest of them, is second magnitude. The other three are third-, fourth-, and fifth-magnitude stars.

There are only three stars that are brighter than Vega. One of them is called *Alpha Centauri,* and is seen in the southern hemisphere. The other two, *Canopus* and Sirius, can be seen in the United States and Canada.

## *MEASURING BRIGHTNESS*

Four different methods are used to measure the brightness of a star. In the first method, the astronomers measure the brightness as it appears to the eye. In the second method, they measure the brightness as it appears on a photograph. In a third method, they measure the brightness by allowing the light to fall on a photoelectric cell. In the fourth method they measure the brightness by allowing the light to fall on a *thermocouple,* an instrument that measures heat. The four measurements usually come out differently. An ordinary photographic plate is not sensitive to red light, but the eye is. So a star that has a lot of red light will seem brighter to the eye than it will on a photograph. The eye is not sensitive to infrared light, but an instrument that measures heat is. So a star that has a lot of infrared light will seem brighter to a heat-measuring instrument than it will to the eye. Because the measurements differ, they are given different names. The measurement by eye is called the *visual magnitude.* The measurement from a photograph is called the *photographic magnitude.* The heat measurement is called the *radiometric magnitude.*

The fact that the four measurements of magnitude come out differently may seem to be a disadvantage. Actually it is an advantage, because the differences between the measurements give us useful information about a star. The difference between the photographic magnitude and the visual magnitude of a star is a clue to how much red light it sends out. This difference is called the *color index* of a star. The difference between the visual magnitude and the radiometric magnitude of a star is a clue to how much infrared light it sends out. Because infrared light is a form of heat, this difference is called the *heat index.* In Chapter 9 we shall see how the color index and the heat index help measure the temperature of a star.

## THE LIGHT ON YOUR BOOK

You may be reading this book by lamplight. If the light on the page is not bright enough, you know you can make it brighter by holding the book closer to the lamp. The closer you are to a lamp, the brighter the light you get from it. The farther away you are, the dimmer the light you get from it. You can see why this is so by looking at the following diagram. The light from the lamp falls on the book. If the book were pulled away, the same light that covers the book would cover the larger space where the shadow of the book now falls on the wall behind it. But when the same amount of light covers a larger space, it is spread out thinner, and so it is dimmer. If the wall is twice as far from the lamp as the book is, the space on the wall is twice as high and twice as wide as the book. We can divide this space into four parts, each as large as the book. Each of these parts would get only one fourth of the light that falls on the book. So the light on the wall would be only one fourth as bright as the light on the book. In other words, when the distance from the lamp is multiplied by 2, the brightness of the light received is divided by 2 times 2. If the wall were three times as far from the lamp as the

book is, the light on the wall would be one ninth as bright as the light on the book. When the distance from the lamp is multiplied by 3, the brightness of the light received is divided by 3 times 3.

Because of this spreading out of light, a bright lamp looks dim if far away. The farther away it is, the dimmer it looks.

## IF THE SUN WERE MOVED

In the daytime the lamp we use is the sun. It is the brightest object in the sky. But if it were farther away than it is, it wouldn't look as bright. If it were moved far enough, it would look no brighter than a star. In fact, if it were one hundred thousand times as far from us as it is, the brightness of the light we receive from it would be divided by 100,000 times 100,000, or 10 thousand million. So at that distance it would look only as bright as the star Sirius. This fact suggests that the stars may really be other suns that are very far away. The suggestion is strengthened by the fact that the spectra of the stars resemble the spectrum of the sun, and show that the stars, like the sun, have hot interiors surrounded by cooler gases.

As we see it in the sky, the sun looks 10 thousand million times as bright as Sirius, but we cannot tell from this fact whether the sun really sends out more light than Sirius does. It is possible that Sirius is just as bright as the sun, or even brighter, but looks dimmer only because it is much farther away. We can't tell how much light it really sends out, compared to the sun, until we know how far away it is.

The amount of light that a star sends out is called its *luminosity,* or its *real brightness.* The brightness that we see when we look at a star in the sky is only how bright it looks from where we are. So it should be called the *apparent brightness,* and its measure is the *apparent magnitude.* The apparent brightness of a star is a clue to its real brightness. But we can't tell from it what the real brightness is until we know the distance to the star.

## CLUES TO DISTANCE

Watch an approaching car coming down a long stretch of road. You can judge its distance by how small it looks to you. The farther away it is, the smaller it looks. This is one of the clues we commonly use for judging distance. But it can't help us measure the distances of the stars. The stars are so far away that when we look at them we see no size at all. Even when we use a telescope, the stars still look like pinpoints of light that cannot be measured. So we have to find some other clue to the distance of the stars.

If, instead of watching a moving car, you ride in one, you will see another way of judging distance. As the car moves down the road, watch the trees in the fields that you pass. They look as though they were all moving the other way. They seem to swing around you in a circle, but not all in the same way. The trees that are near the road seem to move a lot. Those that are farther away seem to move a good deal less. The farther away a tree is, the less it seems to move.

The trees seem to move because the direction in which you see them changes as you move down the road in the car. First you see a tree ahead of you; then you see it at your side; and then you see it behind you. This change in direction is called the *parallax* of the tree. As you move past them, trees that are near have a large parallax, and trees that are far away have a small parallax. So parallax is a clue to distance.

We can use this clue to measure the distances of some stars if we can move ourselves far enough to cause a noticeable shift in the directions of the stars. Fortunately we can, because the earth moves a great distance when it travels in its orbit around the sun. Six months from now we shall be on the other side of the sun, 186 million miles from where we are now. This distance is large enough to allow us to measure the parallax of some stars. The following diagram shows how a star is seen in different directions from opposite sides of the earth's orbit. The distance of the star can be calculated from its parallax.

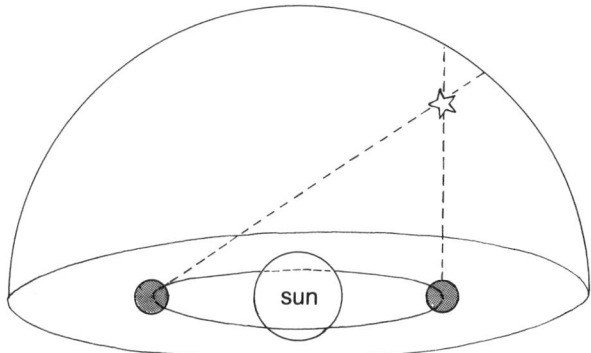

The earth moves around the sun in an ellipse once a year. Because of this motion of the earth, each star seems to make a little ellipse on the sky sphere once a year. The greatest width of this ellipse is the shift in the star's direction as seen first from one place in the earth's orbit and then from the opposite side of the orbit six months later. Astronomers find it more convenient to use half of this width. So the half width of the ellipse the star seems to make is called the parallax of the star. While the earth moves around the sun, the sun itself is moving, carrying the earth's elliptical path with it. Because the earth's ellipse moves, the ellipse the star seems to make moves the other way on the sky sphere. The result is that we don't actually see a closed ellipse. We see a wavy line instead. The following diagram shows a star moving along an ellipse on the sky sphere, while the ellipse moves at the same time. The dotted line shows the wavy path that we see the star follow.

The stars are so far away that their parallaxes are all very small. Every star parallax that has been measured is less than one second of arc on the sky sphere. To measure the parallax of a star from photographs of the sky, astronomers use about twenty photographs taken at different times during two years.

## PARSECS AND LIGHT-YEARS

The stars are so far away that it is inconvenient to measure their distances in miles. Star distances expressed in miles are very big, clumsy numbers. To simplify the arithmetic of star distances, astronomers use a very large unit called the *parsec*. The parsec is the distance a star would have to be from us to have a parallax of one second. When distances are measured in parsecs, the connection between parallax and distance becomes very simple. If a star's parallax is one second, its distance is one parsec. If the parallax is one half of a second, the distance is two parsecs. If the parallax is one third of a second, the distance is three parsecs. The distance of a star is always as many times bigger than a parsec as its parallax is smaller than a second.

In popular articles about the stars, astronomers usually give star distances in *light-years*. A light-year is the distance that light travels in a year. This is a good many miles, since light travels 186,000 miles a second, and there are 60 seconds in a minute, 60 minutes in an hour, 24 hours in a day, and 365¼ days in a year. If you multiply these numbers you will see a light-year is about 6 million million miles. A parsec is about 3¼ times as large as a light-year.

## THE NEAREST STARS

The nearest star is in the constellation *Centaurus* and is known as *Proxima*. It is about 4 light-years away. Sirius, the brightest star in the sky, is about 9 light-years away. By using parallax measurements made on photographs of the sky, astronomers have calculated distances for more than ten thousand stars. The most accurate of these distances are for about seven hundred stars that are less than 65 light-years away. For stars that are more than 300 light-years away, the parallax is so small that it is practically impossible to measure it accurately. So this method of calculating star distances cannot be used for all stars. It is useful only for the nearest ones.

## REAL BRIGHTNESS

By looking at a star, we find out how bright it looks, or

its apparent brightness. By measuring its parallax, we find out how far away it is. From these two facts we can figure out how bright it would look at any other distance. If its distance were half of what it is, for example, it would look four times as bright as it does. If it were three times as far away as it is, it would look only one ninth as bright. But when we know how bright the stars will look at any distance, then we can compare the real brightness of one star with the real brightness of another. All we have to do is figure out how bright they will look when they are both at the same distance from us. If two stars are at the same distance, and one looks brighter than the other, then it really is brighter. The distance used for making this comparison is ten parsecs. The magnitude a star would have if it were ten parsecs away is called the *absolute magnitude* and is a measure of its real brightness.

Since we know the distance of the sun, we can figure out how bright it, too, would look if it were ten parsecs away. Then we can compare the real brightness of other stars with the real brightness of the sun. In this way it was found that if the sun and Sirius were both ten parsecs away, Sirius would look twenty-six times as bright as the sun. So we know that, although the sun looks 10 thousand million times as bright as Sirius, Sirius is really as bright as twenty-six suns put together. Deneb has the brightness of ten thousand suns, and Rigel has the brightness of eighteen thousand suns. Results like these show that the stars are really very bright suns, many of them much brighter than the sun that the earth revolves around. But if the stars are all suns, it means that the sun is a star. Then we can learn a lot about the stars by studying the sun.

## THE SEARCH FOR A TEST LIGHT

We have just seen how it is possible to figure out the real brightness of a star if we know how far away it is. This process can be reversed. If we know how bright a star really is, we can figure out how far away it must be to look as dim as it does. If, for example, we know a certain star is really as bright as the sun, but it looks only one fourth as bright as the sun would if the sun were ten parsecs away, then the star must be twice as far as that, or twenty parsecs away. If the star looks only one ninth as bright, it must be three times ten parsecs away, or thirty parsecs away. The dimmer the star looks, the farther away it must be. So a star of known brightness can serve as a test light that we can use for measuring distance. If we can find such a test light, it will help us measure distances greater than 100 light-years, where the parallax is too small to be of any help. Chapter 8 describes how the astronomers found many such test lights by discovering new ways of recognizing the real brightness of stars.

# 5 The Motion of a Star

## ☆ THE "FIXED" STARS ARE NOT FIXED

The stars have long been known as "fixed" stars because they do not wander around the sky the way the sun, the moon, and the planets do. But actually they are not fixed at all. They do move. There is enough information in the light they send us to help the astronomers figure out how fast they move, and in what directions.

## A STAR'S OWN MOTION

Are *you* moving now? If you are sitting in a chair as you read this book, you would probably say, "No, I'm sitting still." But if someone were out where the sun is, he would say, "That's not so. You *are* moving. I can see you move with the earth, making circles around the earth's axis, and moving along the earth's orbit at the same time." Who is right? You are both right, if we understand what you really mean. When you say you are not moving, you mean you are not moving over the ground. When our imaginary observer on the sun says you *are* moving, he means you are moving past the sun. This shows that a statement that something is moving makes sense only if we answer the question, "Moving past what?" So, to make sense when we speak about the motion of a star, we must begin by answering this question: "Motion past what?" The motion we shall look for in a star is its motion *past* all the other stars put together. Astronomers call this the star's *peculiar motion.* It is the star's own motion as it moves through the crowds of stars that are spread out in the space around us.

## NATURE'S PRACTICAL JOKE

Someone who likes practical jokes once arrived at a birthday party with a tremendous box wrapped in colorful paper and tied with a bright red ribbon. The hostess was thrilled at the sight of a gift box so big, and eagerly began to unwrap it. She removed the ribbon and wrapper and opened the box. Inside she found—another box! When she opened this box, she found that it contained—another box! This went on for many minutes. In every box she opened she found a smaller box inside, until at last in the smallest box she found a pair of earrings.

The peculiar motion of a star is like this pair of earrings. Nature is a practical joker and has hidden it in a box within a box within a box. In order to find it, we have to remove all the boxes, one by one.

## THE STAR'S DAILY CIRCLE

Every star makes a circle around the sky, repeating the trip every day. But this isn't the real motion of the star.

This is only the first box that hides the real motion. A star travels along its daily circle because the whole sky sphere seems to turn. And the sky sphere seems to turn because the earth is rotating on its axis. To get at the gift inside the boxes, we must remove the first box. To find the peculiar motion of a star, astronomers first subtract the effect of the rotation of the earth. What they have left is the way the star seems to move on the sky sphere, apart from the turning of the sky sphere around the earth.

## *SEEING A STAR WHERE IT ISN'T*

As the astronomers watch a star in its place on the sky sphere, they see it shift around a little during the day. It repeats this shifting around in the same way every day. But this shifting is not the real motion of the star. It is only the second box hiding the real motion. It is caused by the air that surrounds the earth.

The earth is surrounded by an ocean of air about six hundred miles deep. The air is piled up in layers of different density. At the bottom, near the ground, the air is dens-

est. There the air particles are crowded together the most. But at higher and higher altitudes the density is lower and lower; that is, the particles are less and less crowded together. The light of a star reaches us only after passing through this ocean of air. But when light passes through layers of different density, it is bent, instead of following a straight path. So, while the starlight enters the air from the direction of the star, it reaches the ground from a different direction. Since we "see" a star in the direction that its light comes from when it strikes our eyes, we then see the star where it isn't.

The bending of starlight by the air is called *refraction*. It is greatest when the star is near the horizon. It is least when the star reaches its highest point in the sky. From what astronomers know about the density of the air at different levels, they can figure out how much the starlight is bent. Then, although they see the star where it isn't, they can figure out where it is. In this way they remove the second box that hides the peculiar motion of the star.

## *THE PARALLAX SHIFT*

Suppose we have removed from the motion of a star the effect of the earth's rotation, and the shifting caused by refraction. The motion that is left is still not the peculiar motion of the star. The peculiar motion is now hidden within a third box, the parallax effect of the earth's yearly trip around the sun. As the earth moves around the sun, each star seems to move the other way on the sky sphere. Because the earth moves along an ellipse, each star traces out a little ellipse in the sky. To uncover a star's peculiar motion, we have to remove the third box by subtracting the yearly parallax motion of the star.

## THE ABERRATION OF LIGHT

The earth's motion around the sun is responsible for a fourth box that hides the peculiar motion of the stars. It is known as the *aberration of light,* another case of seeing a star where it isn't.

Suppose you are riding in a railroad train on a rainy day, and you are watching the rain through the window of the train. If there is no wind, the raindrops will fall straight down to the ground. But it won't look that way to you, because you will be passing the raindrops as they fall. Each raindrop will seem to move toward the rear of the train at the same time that it falls. So the raindrops will seem to follow sloping paths across the window. The direction the raindrops seem to come from is ahead of the overhead direction they really come from.

When we look at a star, the earth is like the moving train, and the starlight is like the falling rain. The motion of the earth makes the starlight seem to come from a different direction, ahead of the true direction of the star. This is the aberration of light. As the earth swings around in its orbit, the aberration of light makes the star shift around in the sky. The aberration shift, like the parallax shift, is repeated once a year.

In any part of the sky, only the nearest stars show a parallax shift that is big enough to be noticed and measured. The amount of parallax depends on how far away a star is, and the farther away the star, the smaller its parallax. But, in the same part of the sky, all the stars will show the same aberration shift, because this depends on the direction but not on the distance from which the starlight comes. Even the faintest, most distant stars, which show no parallax shift at all, will show the full shift caused by the aberration of light. So it is possible to recognize the aberration shift of a star as the yearly shift that it shares with all its close neighbors on the sky sphere. It can also be calculated from the speed of light, the speed of the earth in its orbit, and the direction of the star. Then it can be subtracted from the motion of the star. This removes the fourth box that hides the star's peculiar motion.

## THE VIEW FROM THE SUN

By subtracting parallax and the aberration of light, astronomers remove the effect of the earth's motion around the sun. This is like moving their observatories from the earth to the sun. The motion of the star that remains is the motion as seen from the sun. It is called the star's *proper motion*. The proper motion of a star tells how much it shifts its position on the sky sphere in a year, as seen from the sun. To calculate it, observations made ten, twenty, or even a hundred years apart are used. The longer the time, the more the star has shifted its position and the easier it is to measure how far it has shifted. Proper motions are recorded as a number of seconds of arc per year. The largest-known proper motion belongs to a star of the tenth magnitude, and is about ten seconds per year. The average proper motion of the first-magnitude stars is about one half a second. The average for sixth-magnitude stars is about one sixteenth of a second.

## WHAT PROPER MOTION MEANS

Knowing the proper motion of a star brings us closer to finding its peculiar motion. But there are still a few more boxes to be removed before we find it. To see what the next steps should be, we have to stop here for a while and examine what the proper motion really means.

In the following diagram, the sky sphere is shown as seen from the sun, which is located at *S*. A star is seen on the sky sphere, first at *A*, and one year later at *B*. So *AB* is the amount of its proper motion. It shows a shift of position on the sky sphere. This shift of position shows a

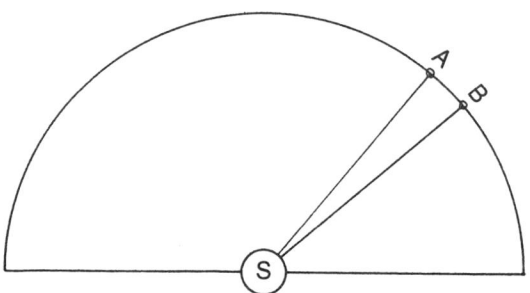

change in direction. First the observer saw the star in the direction *SA*. A year later he saw the star in the direction *SB*. The number of seconds in the arc *AB* tells us the number of seconds in the angle made by the direction line of the star when it turned from position *SA* to position *SB*. This is what the proper motion really means.

## *MOTION IN SPACE*

Now we have to find out the connection between this angle through which the direction line has turned, and the actual motion of the star in space.

The following diagram shows the motion in a year of three different stars. One star moved from *C* to *D*, coming closer to the sun. Its direction line did not turn at all, so this star had no proper motion. If the star moved the other way,

# THE MOTION OF A STAR ☆ 53

from *D* to *C,* so that it was going directly away from the sun, the same thing would be true; the direction line would not turn. No matter how fast a star moves toward the sun or away from the sun, we still see the star in the same direction. So it shows no proper motion on the sky sphere. This means that if a star has no proper motion, so that it keeps its position on the sky sphere, it doesn't prove that the star is not moving. The star may be moving toward the sun or away from the sun. To detect this to or fro motion of a star, some other clue has to be found.

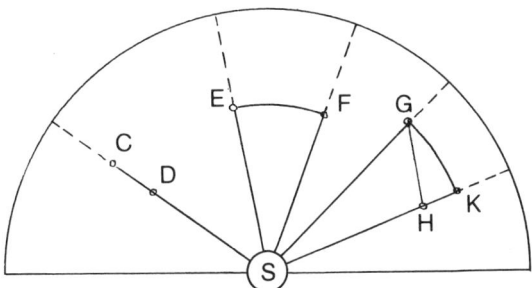

The diagram shows another star that moved from *E* to *F.* This star moved along a circle directly across its direction line, without coming closer to the sun or moving farther away from it. As it moved, its direction line turned from *SE* to *SF.* This shows that proper motion is a clue to motion directly across the direction line.

The third star moved from *G* to *H.* This motion is really a combination of two motions. It's as though it moved across from *G* to *K,* and then moved closer to the sun from *K* to *H.* Of course these two motions do not take place separately, one after the other. They take place at the same time, so that *while* the star moves across, it also moves closer to the sun. But it is helpful to think of them as separate motions. The motion from *G* to *K* is like the motion of the second star from *E* to *F*. It caused a turning of the direction line, so that the proper motion of the star is a clue to this motion across the direction line. The motion from *K* to *H* is like the motion of the first star from *C* to *D*. It caused no turning of the direction line, and so cannot be detected from the proper motion.

Now we can say what the next steps have to be for figuring out the space motion of a star. The space motion of a star is usually like the motion from *G* to *H*. It is made up of two parts: motion across, like *GK;* and motion toward or away from the sun, like *KH*. So we have three steps to take. First we must find a way of figuring out the motion *across.* Next we must find a way of figuring out the motion *toward* or *away* from the sun. Then we must put these two motions together to get the actual *space motion.*

## *MOTION ACROSS*

The following diagram shows once more the motion of a star that moves along a circle across its direction line. *EF* is the actual distance it moves in a year. As it moves

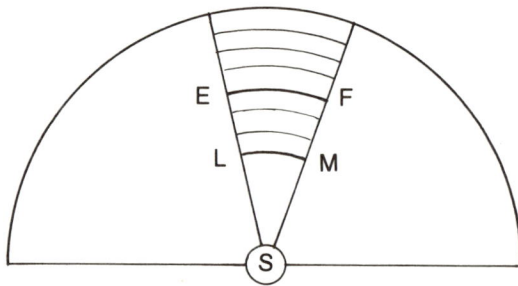

across this distance, its direction line turns from *SE* to *SF*. The amount of this turning is the angle between *SE* and *SF*, and this is its proper motion. Now if the star were closer to the sun and moved from *L* to *M* instead of from *E* to *F*, its proper motion would still be the same, because *L* and *E* have the same direction line, and *M* and *F* have the same direction line. So even if we know the proper motion, which tells us how much the direction line has turned, we cannot tell whether the star moved from *E* to *F*, or from *L* to *M*. In fact, we would have a whole family of motions to choose from, made up of all the circular lines that cross over from the line *SE* to the line *SF* without getting closer to or farther away from the sun. To make the correct choice, we would have to know how far away the star is from the sun. If the distance of the star from the sun is *SE*, then *EF* is the distance the star moved in a year. If the distance of the star from the sun is *SL*, then *LM* is the distance the star moved in a year. This shows that when the proper motion of a star is known, and the distance to the star is also known, the star's motion across the direction line can be measured. The astronomers find it from a calculation that takes the place of the diagram we have been looking at. Our diagram also shows that when two stars have the same proper motion, the nearer star of the two actually has a smaller crosswise motion than the one that is farther away. *(LM is smaller than EF.)*

## TO OR FRO MOTION

The proper motion of a star gives no hint of the star's motion toward or away from the sun. So we have to look for another clue to help us. We find this clue in a common experience that everybody has had.

If an automobile speeds past you while sounding its horn, listen to the tone of the horn. As the car approaches you, the tone is high. Then, immediately after the car passes you, the tone drops, and it doesn't sound like the same horn at all. But it is the same horn, and the change in tone is easy to explain. The sound of the horn is a vibration of the air caused by a vibration in the horn that gives the air a series of pushes one after the other. These pushes or pulses travel through the air at a speed of about eleven hundred feet a second. The distance that a pulse travels in the time between one pulse and the next is the wavelength of the sound. So each pulse is one wavelength ahead of the pulse that follows it. What the tone sounds like depends on how big this wavelength is. High tones have a short wavelength. Low tones have a long wavelength.

Now look at the next three drawings. The first sketch shows a car that is standing still while the driver is blowing the horn. The boy at the left is listening to the sound.

The first two pulses that he will hear are shown where they would be at the moment the second pulse leaves the horn. The distance between the two pulses is the wavelength of the sound. This is how far the first pulse traveled

between pulses the first pulse would still travel the same distance as before. But meanwhile the car has been moving backward, away from it. This carries the second pulse away from the first, so the distance between them is made longer. With a longer wavelength, the sound has a lower tone. So, if a sounding horn is moving away from you, it has a lower tone than if it were standing still. When a car passes you with its horn sounding, first the car is moving toward you, and then it is moving away from you. As it moves toward you, the horn has a higher tone than usual. Then, as it moves away from you, the horn has a lower tone than usual. That is why the tone drops suddenly after the car passes you.

The clue for the astronomers lies in the fact that you can recognize if a horn is moving toward you or away from you by the change in the tone of its sound. A star doesn't send us any sound, but it does send us light, which is also a vibration. The motion of the star has the same effect on its light that the motion of the horn has on its sound. When the star moves toward us, the wavelength of every color in its light is made shorter. This moves all the colors and all the dark lines in its spectrum towards the violet end. When the star moves away from us, the wavelength of every color in its light is made longer. This moves all the colors and all the dark lines in its spectrum toward the red end. This shifting of the spectrum toward either the violet or the red end is known as the *Doppler effect.* We know that astronomers can recognize the dark lines in the spectrum as fingerprints of certain elements. From laboratory studies they know just where to find them in the spectrum. Then, if they find the lines in the wrong place in the spectrum of a star, shifted toward either end of the spectrum,

## THE MOTION OF A STAR

in the time between pulses. The second sketch shows w[hat] would happen if the car were moving toward the boy [in]stead of standing still. In the time between pulses, the f[irst]

pulse would still travel the same distance as before. [But] meanwhile the car has been following it. This brings [the] second pulse closer to the first pulse, so the distance [be]tween them is shorter. But this distance is the wavele[ngth] of the sound. With a shorter wavelength, the sound h[as a] higher tone. So, if a sounding horn is moving toward [you,] it has a higher tone than if it were standing still.

The third sketch shows what would happen if th[e car] were backing up, moving away from the boy. In the

the shift of the lines is a message. If the lines are shifted toward the violet end of the spectrum, the astronomers know that the star is moving toward us and the sun. If the lines are shifted toward the red end of the spectrum, they know that the star is moving away from us and the sun. From the amount of the shift they can figure out how fast the star is moving toward or away from us.

## *SPACE MOTION*

We know now that the motion of a star directly across its direction line can be calculated from its proper motion (change of direction in a year as seen from the sun) and its distance. We also know that its motion toward the sun or away from the sun can be calculated from the change in color of the dark lines in its spectrum. Now we have to put these two motions together to make the combined space motion of the star. This can be done by means of the following simple diagram.

Suppose we have found that a star is moving across its direction line at a speed of 9 miles per second, and it is moving toward the sun at a speed of 12 miles per second.

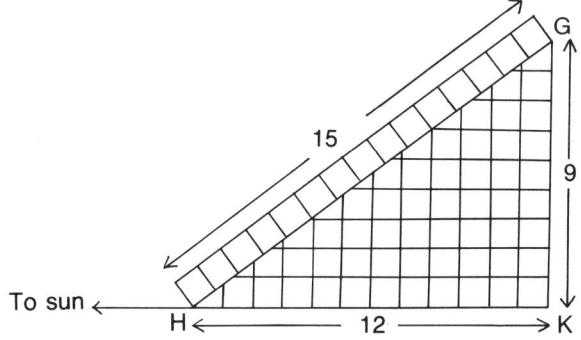

On graph paper draw an arrow *GK* nine boxes long to represent the motion across the direction line *KH*. Now draw the arrow *KH* twelve boxes long on the direction line. Now join *G* to *H*. The arrow *GH* represents the space motion of the star. The length of *GH*, measured on the scale of the graph paper, represents the speed of this space motion. In this case it is 15 miles per second, as you can tell by laying the length *GH* down on a horizontal line of the graph paper and then counting the boxes. The direction of *GH* shows the actual direction of the space motion of the star. In practice, astronomers do not find the space motion from a diagram. They find it by a calculation that does the same thing as the diagram. The calculation uses the rule of Pythagoras, which you learn when you study elementary algebra.

## *THE MOTION OF THE SUN*

The three steps we took to find the space motion of the star removed three more boxes that were hiding the star's peculiar motion. But we haven't found this peculiar motion yet. The space motion of the star tells us only how it moves as seen from the sun. If a star is seen to be approaching the sun, it may mean that the star is moving toward the sun. But it may also mean that the sun is moving toward the star. The space motion of the star is a combination of the peculiar motion of the star and the peculiar motion of the sun. So we have one more box to remove. To find the peculiar motion of the star, we have to remove that part of the space motion of the star that comes from the motion of the sun. Before we can do this, we have to know what the sun's motion is.

The clue to the sun's motion comes from another

familiar experience. Suppose you are standing on a crowded beach. You are surrounded by people on all sides. People are moving helter-skelter in all directions. Some are walking; some are running; others are jumping. No matter which way you look, you see as many people moving in one direction as in any other direction. But if you start moving through the crowd in a straight line, then what you see is changed. Although the people still move helter-skelter in all directions, your own motion is now combined with theirs, and you see them streaming past you on both sides. People ahead of you seem to approach you, glide past at your side, and then move away behind you. The direction in which the crowd seems to be streaming is the opposite of the direction in which you are walking. The speed of the streaming is the speed with which you are walking. Here is the clue that we needed. As seen from the sun, the stars are moving helter-skelter in all directions. At the same time they tend to stream past us in one special direction, like a river flowing past an anchored boat. From this streaming of the stars, the astronomers know that the sun is really moving in the opposite direction. The speed of the sun's motion is 13 miles per second. It is moving in the direction of the star Vega, brightest star in the constellation Lyra.

## *PECULIAR MOTION OF A STAR*

Now we can remove the last box that hides a star's peculiar motion. We subtract the motion of the sun from the space motion of the star. What is left is the star's peculiar motion, its own motion among the crowds of surrounding stars. To find it, we had to remove eight boxes in which it came wrapped.

# 6 Sky Families

## ☆ STARS THAT MOVE TOGETHER

MOST stars that are seen in the same part of the sky have no connection with each other. They are seen together because they happen to be in about the same direction from us. But their proper motions show that they are going their separate ways, in different directions and at different speeds. But there are exceptions to this rule. Here and there in the sky we see groups of stars whose proper motions show that they are moving together. They are called *moving clusters.* The Hyades, in the constellation Taurus, form a moving cluster.

The following diagram shows how the Hyades would shift their positions in the sky, as seen from the sun, during a period of fifty thousand years. Each arrow shows the amount and direction of the proper motion of one star in that time. Notice how all the little arrows point to the same place in the sky. It looks as if the stars in the cluster had an appointment to meet there and were all rushing to that place to keep the appointment. If this were really so, they would be headed for a terrible collision. But they are not actually headed for a smashup. This is only an optical illusion. You have the same illusion whenever you look at straight railroad tracks. Straight railroad tracks lying side by side look as though they meet somewhere in the distance. But we know they don't really meet. They look as though they meet because they are parallel, or point in the same direction. If we draw a line from our eyes toward the place where the tracks seem to meet, this line runs in the same direction as the tracks. The same thing is true of the motion of the Hyades. They look as though they will meet because they are all moving in the same direction. If we draw a line from the sun toward the place where the proper motions seem to meet, this line points out the direction in which the cluster is moving.

In some clusters, the proper motions of the stars give a different kind of illusion. The lines of the proper motions all come together at one point in the sky, but the stars all

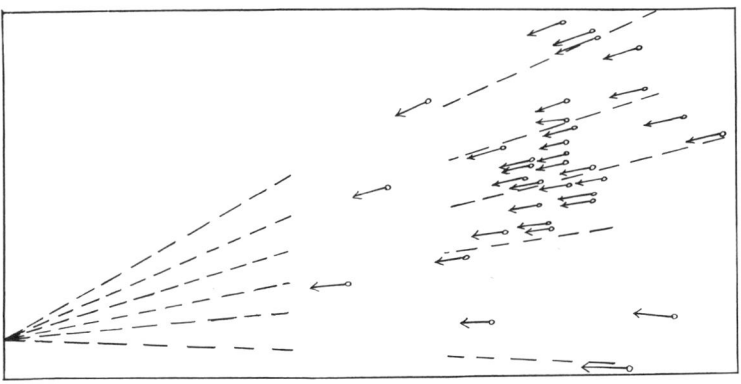

seem to be headed away from that point. They look like flying fragments shooting away from the scene of a great explosion. But they are not really coming from the same point. They are coming from the same direction. A line from the sun to the point in the sky that they seem to be coming from points out the direction from which the cluster is moving. Stars in a cluster that is moving away from us seem to be heading *toward* one point in the sky. Stars in a cluster that is moving toward us seem to be heading *away* from one point in the sky.

## SOME MOVING CLUSTERS

The Pleiades, like the Hyades, are a moving cluster. Another well-known moving cluster includes five of the stars in the Big Dipper. The star Sirius, although it is in a different part of the sky, belongs to the same cluster as these Dipper stars.

The red star Antares and other stars of the constellation Scorpius are part of a large moving cluster that includes stars from Centaurus and the Southern Cross (constellations of the southern hemisphere). There is a moving cluster in Perseus, and another in Orion.

## SPINNING TWINS

The star Albireo is the foot of the Northern Cross in the constellation Cygnus. If you look at it through a pair of powerful binoculars, or through a telescope, it turns out to be two stars instead of one. One of the stars is golden yellow, and the other one is blue. They lie so close to each other on the sky sphere that they look like a single star to the naked eye. Double stars like Albireo are called *binaries*.

# SKY FAMILIES ☆ 65

In Chapter 2 we saw that some stars are seen near each other on the sky sphere, even though they aren't close to each other in space at all. They seem close only because we see them in almost the same direction. Since they have no connection with each other, they usually have different proper motions. But there are other stars that really are close to each other. They are twin stars, and they have about the same proper motion. In addition, as they move along together, each pulls on the other with the force of gravitation. Because of this pull they spin around each other like partners in a dance. Each one moves around the other along an elliptical path in the same way that the earth revolves around the sun. By noticing how the fainter of the two stars shifts around the brighter one from year to year, we can actually see its orbit as it looks on the sky sphere. The following diagram shows how one of the stars in a typical binary moved around its partner between the

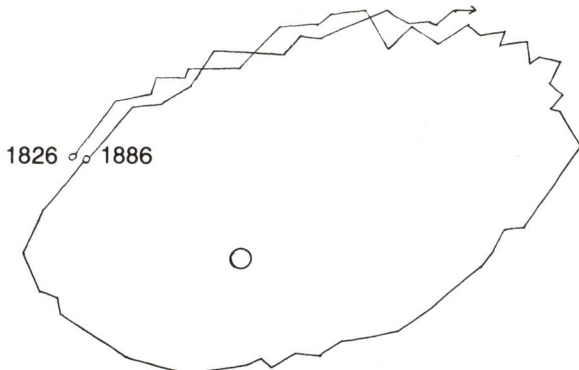

years 1826 and 1886. It took sixty years to make a round trip. The bright star Sirius has a faint companion that revolves around it once every fifty years.

## TILTED ORBITS

The rim of a plate is a circle. But we don't always see it as a circle. If we look at it from above, it looks like a circle. If we look at it at an angle, it looks like an ellipse. The more it is tilted toward our eyes, the narrower the ellipse becomes. If we look at it edgewise, it looks like a straight line. So the shape we see isn't always the true shape of the rim of the plate.

The orbit of a star around its twin is like the rim of a plate. If we look at it from above, we see its true shape. But if the orbit is tilted toward us, so that we see it at an angle, then the shape we see is different from the true shape of the orbit. If we look at the orbit edgewise, it looks like a straight line, and the star seems to move back and forth along this line.

## TWINS WE CAN'T SEPARATE

Most stars that look double in a telescope look single to the naked eye. Our eyes alone are not powerful enough to separate the light of the twins so that we may see them as a pair. The farther away the twins are from us, the harder it is to see them separately. But this means that if binaries are far enough away, our telescopes won't separate them either, and they will still look like single stars.

SKY FAMILIES ☆ 67

Fortunately there are ways of recognizing double stars even when they look single. One of these ways makes use of the spectrum of the stars.

Suppose the orbit that a star follows around its twin is tilted toward us. The following diagram shows what its path would look like. The arrows show the direction in

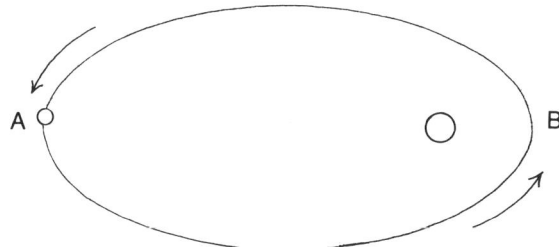

which the star is moving. Because the orbit is tilted toward us, when the star is at *A* it is moving toward us. When the star is at *B,* it is moving away from us. But when it moves toward us, the lines in its spectrum will be shifted toward the violet. When it moves away from us, the lines will be shifted toward the red. This shifting of the lines in the spectrum may be seen even if the stars are too far away to be seen in the telescope as a pair. In some stars, recognized as binaries in this way, only the spectrum of the brighter of the two stars is seen. In others, the spectra of both stars are seen, so that the spectrum of the binary has a double set of lines. As the stars swing around each other, there are times when one star is moving toward us while the other star is moving away from us. At these times, one set of lines in the spectrum shifts toward the violet while the other set shifts toward the red.

Double stars that can be seen separately through a telescope are called *visual binaries*. Double stars that are recognized from the Doppler shift in the spectrum are called *spectroscopic binaries*. The study of spectroscopic binaries has shown that most stars are double, and some are even triple or quadruple. The single star that wanders through space alone is the exception, not the rule.

## ECLIPSING STARS

There are some binaries which revolve around each other in orbits that we see edgewise. The following diagram shows a star moving along such an orbit around its twin. Because we see the orbit edgewise, it looks as though the star moves back and forth along a straight line. First

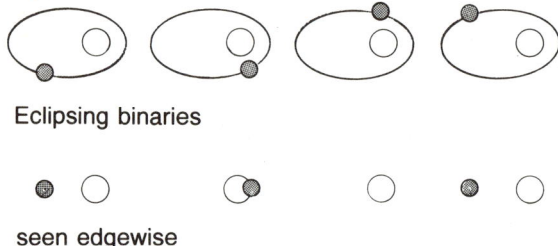

Eclipsing binaries

seen edgewise

it passes in front of its twin, then swings around and passes behind it. But when one star is in front of the other, it cuts off the light of the star behind it and prevents that light from reaching us. As a result, the amount of light that we get from the pair goes through a series of changes as the star makes a round trip in its orbit. We get the most light when the two stars are side by side, and we see them both. The amount of light drops when the fainter star passes in front of the brighter one. The amount of light increases again after the star has passed before its twin, and both stars can be seen again. It drops again, but not so much as before, when the faint star passes behind the bright one. It increases again when the two are side by side once more. We see these changes as variations or changes in the brightness of the pair. The changes are repeated regularly during every round trip the stars make around each other. Pairs of stars that block off each other's light in this way are called *eclipsing binaries.* Algol, the blinking star in Perseus that the Arabs called the Demon, is an eclipsing binary.

Eclipsing pairs can be recognized even if the stars are so far away that the pair looks like a single star. They are identified by the way the brightness changes. The pair has its greatest brightness most of the time. Then the brightness drops suddenly only for the short time when one star is behind the other. These changes in brightness are also accompanied by shifts in the lines of the spectrum. As one star revolves around the other, first it moves toward us, so that the lines shift toward the violet. Then, as it begins to pass in front of the other star, the lines are in their usual place. Next, as it swings around, it moves away from us, and the lines shift toward the red. When it begins to pass behind the other star, the lines are in their usual place again. The lines in the spectrum of an eclipsing binary shift back and forth with the same rhythm with which the brightness changes.

## STARS THAT THROB

The star Delta Cephei changes in brightness with a regular rhythm. It increases in brightness for a day, and then drops in brightness gradually during the next 4½ days. It repeats the same changes every 5½ days. The lines in its spectrum also shift back and forth with the same rhythm. But Delta Cephei is not an eclipsing binary, because the brightness changes, and the lines shift in the wrong way. An eclipsing binary is bright most of the time, then drops in brightness suddenly for a short time only. But the brightness of Delta Cephei drops gradually. In an eclipsing binary, when the lines of the spectrum shift toward the violet, the pair is brightest. When the lines shift toward the red, the pair is brightest again. There is no shift when the pair is dimmest. But in Delta Cephei, while the lines shift to the violet when the star is brightest, they shift to the red when the star is dimmest.

Since Delta Cephei cannot be an eclipsing binary, astronomers had to find another explanation for the regular changes in its brightness and its spectrum. The theory that seems to fit the facts best is that the star is throbbing, first swelling up like a balloon being blown up, and then growing smaller like a balloon from which air is escaping. As it expands, its surface moves toward us, so the lines in the spectrum shift toward the violet. As it contracts, its surface pulls away from us, so the lines in the spectrum shift toward the red.

Stars that change in brightness the way Delta Cephei does are called *Cepheid variables.* The time that it takes for a complete cycle of changes is called the *period* of the star. Hundreds of Cepheids have been studied. They don't all have the same period. Their periods range from 1 day to 50 days.

## STARS THAT FLARE UP

In November 1572, a star suddenly appeared in the sky where none had been seen before. It grew in brightness until it was so bright it could be seen in the daytime. Then it gradually grew fainter. After sixteen months it couldn't be seen any more. People called it a *nova,* or "new" star. Many novae have been seen since then. But now that we have telescopes and have taken photographs of the sky, we know that they are not new stars. They are stars that were there all the time but were too faint to be seen by the naked eye. They attracted attention when they suddenly became about a thousand times as bright as they were at first. Then they became faint again. Many astronomers think that nearly all novas are small, dense, white members of a binary pair whose companion is large, bright, red, and rarified—that is, with its mass spread out thinly in a big space. One is a white dwarf, and the other is a red giant, as described in Chapter 9. The dwarf flares up when it captures some gas from its giant companion. The captured mass causes a burst of energy that suddenly brightens the star.

Photographs of novae taken over a period of years show that a nova is a star that has thrown out a mass of gas. The gas forms a shell-like cloud surrounding the star.

Expanding cloud of gas around Nova Persei. The gas was thrown out of the star in 1901, and has been rushing away from it ever since. HALE OBSERVATORIES

The shell expands as the gas rushes away from the star in all directions. The part of the shell that faces us is rushing toward us. The light of the star passes through this part of the shell before it reaches us. The lines in its spectrum show a shift toward the violet. From this shift the astronomers figure out how fast the shell-like cloud of gas is expanding.

## EXPLODING STARS

Some stars flare up to over a million times their original brightness. These are called *supernovae.* They are stars that have exploded and thrown out a great mass of gas. The Crab Nebula is a shell-like cloud of gas thrown out by a star that exploded in 1054. (*Nebula* is the Latin word for cloud.)

The Crab Nebula, in the constellation Taurus, is the wreckage of a star that exploded in the year 1054. HALE OBSERVATORIES

a

b

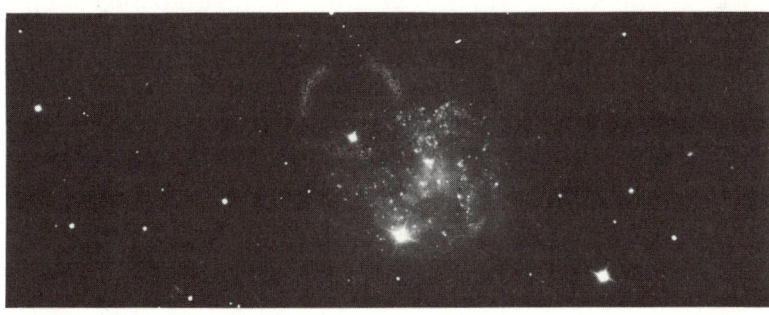

c

Three views of a supernova: a. 1937, b. 1938, c. 1942 (too faint to observe) HALE OBSERVATORIES

## THE MILKY WAY

As seen by the naked eye, the Milky Way looks like a narrow cloud stretched across the sky. When it is viewed through a powerful telescope, however, the Milky Way is seen to be a great family of stars. There are over 100,000 million stars in the Milky Way. The sun and all the stars we can see with the naked eye are among them. The Milky Way is also called the *Galaxy* (spelled with a capital *G*), a name that comes from the Greek word for milk.

Astronomers have found out the positions and motions of many of the stars in the Galaxy by studying the light that comes from them. Some stars in the Galaxy are behind great clouds of gas and dust in space. Although the dust clouds block the light that comes from these stars, they do not block the radio waves that come from them. By putting together information obtained from the light and the radio waves that come from different parts of the Galaxy, astronomers have figured out the size and shape of the Galaxy and how it moves.

The Galaxy is shaped like a big wheel with a bulge at the middle where the hub of the wheel would be. Extending out from this bulge and surrounding it are three spiral arms. The diameter of the Galaxy is about 80,000 light-years. The core of the galaxy, which makes up the bulge at the center, is about 30,000 light-years wide. The thickness of the bulge is about 15,000 light-years. The thickness of each spiral arm is only about 1,000 light-years.

The three spiral arms of the Galaxy are named after constellations that are in them. The inner arm is called the *Sagittarius arm*. The middle arm is the *Orion arm*. The outer arm, called the *Perseus arm,* is actually a continuation of the Sagittarius arm. The sun is near the inner edge of the middle arm at a distance of 30,000 light-years from the center of the Galaxy.

It has been known since 1927 that the Galaxy is spinning like a top. Stars nearer the core take less time for a

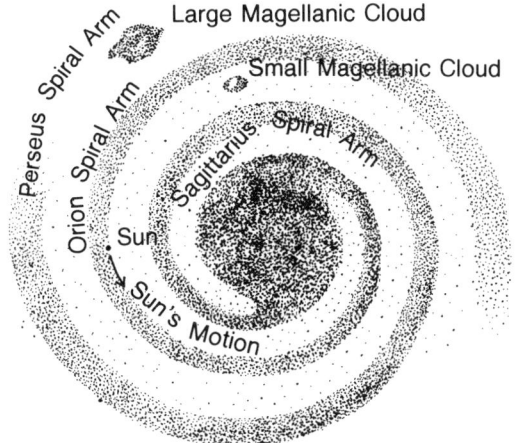

The Milky Way, top view

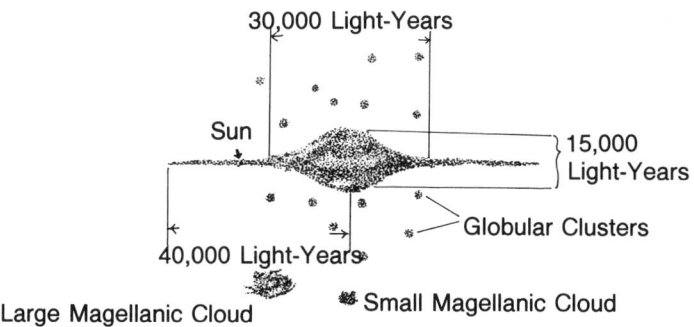

The Milky Way as seen edge-on, with its halo of globular clusters and its nearest neighbors

round trip around the core than stars that are farther away from it. The sun completes a round trip in 250 million years.

## GLOBULAR CLUSTERS

Tens of thousands of stars lie between us and the center of the Galaxy and prevent us from seeing it. For this reason an indirect method had to be used to find out where the center of the Galaxy is. The clue that first helped astronomers locate the center was found in the *globular clusters* of the Galaxy. Each globular cluster is a ball-shaped group of stars containing between a hundred thousand and a million stars. There are about one hundred of them scattered through the Galaxy, and they surround the center of the Galaxy like a halo. The center of the Galaxy is the center of this halo. There are Cepheid variables in the globular clusters. Applying a method to be described later in Chapter 8, astronomers were able to use these Cepheid variables to measure the distance from the earth to each globular cluster. Then, knowing where the globular clusters are, they located the center around which they form a halo.

## OUTSIDE THE GALAXY

There are some patches of light in the sky that are called clouds or nebulae because they look like clouds, but they aren't clouds at all. The most conspicuous of these are the two Magellanic Clouds that can be seen in the southern hemisphere. Another, also visible to the naked eye, is the Great Nebula in Andromeda. There are many others, visible only through a telescope. The distances to these nebulae have been measured by methods described in

Chapter 7. The distances show that these nebulae lie outside the Galaxy, and are in fact great families of stars like the Galaxy itself. For this reason they are called *galaxies* (with a small *g*). The Galaxy which contains our sun is only one of a multitude of galaxies scattered throughout space.

## *RUNAWAY GALAXIES*

The galaxies are scattered through space as far as our largest telescopes can see. The telescopes catch enough light from the nearer ones (up to a few thousand million light-years away) to spread out in a spectrum. Study of

The 200-inch Hale telescope on Mount Palomar HALE
OBSERVATORIES

these spectra uncovered one of the strangest facts of astronomy. The lines of the spectra of all but a few nearby galaxies are shifted toward the red. This means that these galaxies are moving away from us. The lines also show that the farther away a galaxy is, the faster it is moving away. A galaxy that is 12 million light-years away runs away from us at a speed of 180 miles a second. One that is 90 million light-years away flees at a speed of 1,350 miles a second. A galaxy 720 million light-years away recedes at a speed of 10,800 miles a second. It is as if some great explosion sent them all flying apart. If there were such an explosion in the past—and there is evidence for it—it must have happened about 17,000 million years ago, for this is the amount of time it would have taken the galaxies to reach the places they are in now.

# 7 Weighing the Stars

## ☆ THE BABY AND THE MAN

It is easy to give a baby a ride on a sled. If you pull on the sled ever so lightly, the sled begins to move. But if you had to give a man a ride, it would not be so easy. You would have to pull very hard before the sled would move. That is because the man is heavier, or has more *mass,* than the baby. The more mass a body has, the harder it is to make it move. Then, once it is moving, the more mass a body has, the harder it is to stop it or make it turn. The mass of a body makes it resist any change in its motion. This rule gives us a hint on how we might weigh a star. To weigh a star, we have to push it or pull it, and see how hard it resists being pushed or pulled. But then we have a little problem to solve: How do we manage to push or pull a star?

## THE PULL OF THE EARTH

We can get a clue to how we might weigh a star by

remembering how we weigh things here on the earth. To weigh a bag of potatoes, we put it on a scale. The potatoes press down on the scale, and the pointer shows us how hard they press down. The heavier the potatoes are, or the more mass they have, the harder they press down. This happens because the earth is pulling on the potatoes. The earth pulls on all things that are near it. The heavier a thing is, the harder it is pulled.

## PULLING A STAR

Just as the earth pulls on all things that are near it, the sun and the stars pull on things that are near them. They pull with a strength that depends on their own mass. The heavier a star is, the harder it pulls. When two stars are close to each other, as in binary stars, they pull on each other. Here is the pull we can use to help us weigh the stars. It is known as the *force of gravitation.*

## DANCING PARTNERS

Suppose two dancers stand toe to toe, grasp hands, lean back, and spin around each other. If they let go, they would fall away from each other. They would separate because there is a force that is trying to pull them apart. This force arises because the mass of each dancer resists the turning which keeps changing the direction in which the dancer moves. It is called the *centrifugal force* (force pulling away from the center), and its strength depends on how heavy the dancers are. But as long as they hold hands, they pull toward each other, too. This pull balances the centrifugal force. So instead of flying apart, they keep swinging around each other.

The earth and the sun are like dancing partners. As

the earth swings around the sun, the centrifugal force tries to pull them apart. But, at the same time, the earth and the sun pull toward each other with the force of gravitation. The force of gravitation balances the centrifugal force. So the earth and the sun do not fly apart, and the earth keeps swinging around the sun. Each of the planets is kept swinging around the sun in the same way. Physicists have found that the time that it takes for a planet to make a trip around the sun depends on its distance from the sun and on how heavy the sun and the planet are together.

Binary stars are also like dancing partners. As they swing around each other, the centrifugal force tries to pull them apart. But it is balanced by the force of gravitation with which the two stars pull toward each other. The balance of these two forces keeps the twin stars swinging around and around each other. The time that it takes for them to make one round trip depends on how far apart the stars are, and on how heavy they are. The time for one round trip is called the *period* of the motion of the stars.

## WEIGHING A STAR BY ITS MOTION

The first stars to be weighed were visual binaries, whose distance from us had already been calculated from their parallax. They were weighed by comparing their motions with the motion of the earth around the sun. The mathematical formulas that describe the balance between the force of gravitation and the centrifugal force show exactly how the mass of the stars is connected with their distance from each other and with their period. They show that, if the twin stars have the same period as the earth (one year) but are twice as far apart as the earth and sun, then their combined mass is 2 x 2 x 2, or eight times the combined mass of the earth and sun. If they are three times as far apart as the earth and sun, then their combined mass is 3 x 3 x 3, or twenty-seven times the combined mass of the earth and sun. If the distance between the twin stars is the same as the distance between the earth and the sun, but their period is two years, then the mass of the stars is equal to the mass of the earth and sun divided by 2 x 2, or four. If the period is three years, then the mass of the stars is equal to the mass of the earth and sun divided by 3 x 3, or nine. To find the combined mass of any twin stars, you multiply the combined mass of the earth and sun three times by the number of times the distance between the earth and sun would fit into the distance between the stars. Then you divide twice by the number of years in the period of the stars.

To make this calculation, the astronomers must first know the period of the stars (how long it takes the stars to turn around each other once), and how far apart they are. The astronomers measure the period directly as they watch the stars make a round trip. To find out how far apart the stars are, they first measure their separation on the sky sphere. This separation is the proper motion one of the stars would have if we imagine it moving to where the other star is. The explanation in Chapter 5 showed how the distance between the two positions is found from the angle between their direction lines and the distance of the stars from the sun.

The star Sirius and its companion have a period of fifty years. The average distance between them is about twenty times the distance between the earth and the sun. So their combined mass is about 20 x 20 x 20 times the combined mass of the sun and the earth divided by 50 x 50. Since the mass of the sun alone is almost the same as the mass of the sun and the earth combined, this shows that, together, Sirius and its companion weigh almost 3½ times as much as the sun. By watching the motion of each of the twins separately, the astronomers also know how the two stars share this mass. The clue they use is the fact that the heavier of the two stars moves more slowly. Sirius alone is about 2½ times as heavy as the sun. Its companion has the same mass as the sun.

## *MASS AND REAL BRIGHTNESS*

After measuring the mass of many visual binaries, the astronomers discovered an interesting and important fact. The heavier a star is, the brighter it shines. This rule is shown in the following chart. In this chart, each dot stands

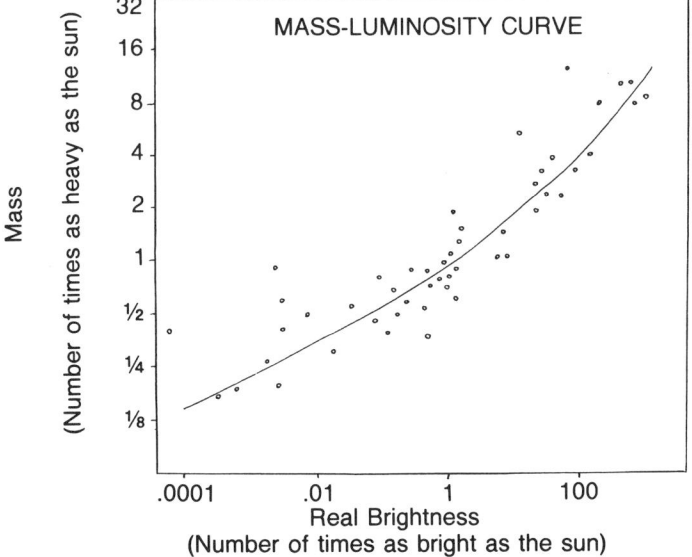

for a star that has been weighed. The stars are arranged from left to right in the order of their real brightness. The faintest stars are at the left, and the brightest are at the right. At the same time they are arranged from bottom to top in the order of their mass. Those with smallest mass are at the bottom. The heaviest stars are at the top. Notice how they all cluster around the line that goes from the lower left-hand corner to the upper right-hand corner of the chart. This line is known as the *mass-luminosity curve*.

## SQUEEZING LIGHT FROM A STAR

The connection between the mass and the brightness of the double stars is not an accident. It can be explained by the known facts and laws of physics. The gas in a star is all pulled toward the center of the star by the force of gravitation. The mass of the outer layers of gas presses down on the gas near the center. This compresses the center and makes it hot enough to glow. At the high temperature that is produced, part of the mass of the star is turned into light and heat by a process like that in the H-bomb. The more mass the star has, the more strongly its gases are pulled toward the center. The harder they are pulled, the more they squeeze the center. The more the center is squeezed, the higher the pressure in it, the hotter it gets, and the more light and heat are produced. Meanwhile, the high pressure at the center of the star pushes outward. The escaping light and heat also push outward. These outward pushes balance the inward pull of gravitation and keep the star from collapsing.

## WEIGHING A STAR BY ITS LIGHT

The theory of how a star's own mass squeezes light out of it explains why twin stars shine. But it also explains why all other stars shine. This means that the connection between mass and brightness must be true for all stars, and not only for double stars. When they recognized this fact, the astronomers had a means of weighing a star by its light. Here is how it is done. By measuring the apparent brightness of a star, and its parallax, we can figure out the star's real brightness. This was explained in Chapter 4. But if you know the real brightness of a star, the mass-luminosity curve tells you how heavy the star is. Suppose, for example, a star is as bright as 100 suns. Place your finger over the number 100 at the bottom of the mass-luminosity chart. Move your finger up toward the top of the chart until you reach the line around which the dots cluster. Then move your finger to the left. It will point to the number 4, showing that the star is four times as heavy as the sun. By using the mass-luminosity curve you can get the mass of any star, even if it is not a binary, as long as you know how far away it is.

# 8 Overlapping Yardsticks

## ☆ MANY YARDSTICKS

Measuring the parallax of stars gives astronomers a kind of yardstick for measuring the distances to the stars, as we saw in Chapter 4. But this yardstick can measure distances no farther than 300 light-years. To measure beyond 300 light-years astronomers had to find other yardsticks. By using many different clues that are found in the light of the stars, astronomers have developed a system of overlapping yardsticks reaching out to different distances that permits them to measure distances as great as a few thousand million light-years. Where two yardsticks overlap, the measuring scale on the shorter one can be transferred to the longer one. Then the longer one can be used to make measurements to a greater distance into space.

## THE DISTANCE OF MOVING CLUSTERS

The stars in a moving cluster seem to be headed toward or away from one point in the sky. This point shows us the direction in which all the stars in the cluster are moving. But when we know this direction, we can figure out the distance of each star in the cluster without measuring its parallax. The following diagrams show how this is done. In diagram *A,* the arrow shows the direction in which we see the star as seen from the sun. In diagram *B,* another arrow has been put in, showing the direction in which the star is moving together with its companions in the cluster. This is the direction of the space motion of the

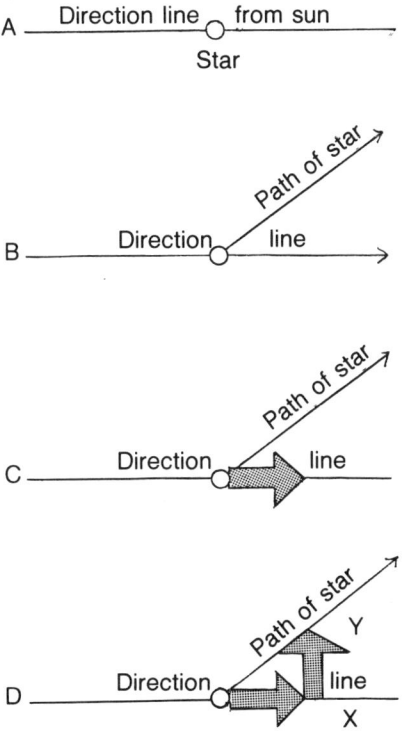

star and is the actual path that it follows. In Chapter 5 we found that the space motion of a star is made up of two parts. One is the motion toward or away from the sun. The other is the motion across the direction line of the star. We can calculate the motion of the star toward or away from the sun by the Doppler shift of the lines in its spectrum. In diagram *C,* a short arrow has been placed on the direction line of the star to show how far it moves away from the sun in a year. In diagram *D,* another arrow, labeled *XY,* has been put in, showing how far the star must move across the direction line in the same time in order to stay on its path. The length of the arrow *XY* shows the actual distance it moves across its direction line in a year.

The star's motion across its direction line in a year makes it shift its position on the sky sphere. As it shifts on the sky sphere its direction line turns. The angle through which the direction line turns in a year is the proper motion of the star and can be measured. It is shown in diagram *E.* In diagram *F,* the length *XY* is placed across the

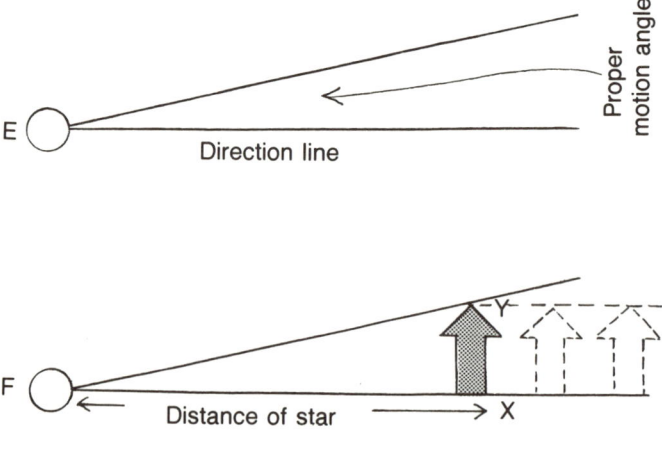

figure *F* on the preceding page. They do it by means of the calculation that takes the place of the diagram. The distance they get in this way has to be corrected, because it was based on guessing the masses of the stars.

Step 3. They measure the apparent brightness of each of the twin stars. Then, using the distance they found in Step 2, they calculate the real brightness of each star, as explained on page 44 of Chapter 4.

Step 4. From Step 3 astronomers know the real brightness of each of the twin stars. Now, using the mass-luminosity curve, they find out the mass of each. In this way they get a better measure of the masses than the guess that they started with. Using this corrected measure of the mass, they start all over again with Step 1. They repeat the series of steps several times, each time getting a more accurate measure of the mass when they complete Step 4, and a more accurate measure of the distance the next time they complete Step 2. The corrections grow smaller and smaller until the best answer is reached.

## CHECK AND DOUBLE CHECK

Sometimes more than one method can be used for measuring the distance of a star. If the star is not too far away, the parallax method can be used. If the star is also in a moving cluster, the cluster method can be used. If the star is one of a pair of spinning twins, the orbit method can be used. Where more than one method is used, each one serves as a check on the others. The astronomers are doubly sure their measurements are right when all the different methods give them the same result.

direction line and moved into the position where it just reaches across the opening of the proper-motion angle. When $XY$ is in this position, the line from $X$ to the sun shows the distance of the star. In practice, the astronomers find it from a calculation that takes the place of these diagrams.

When the distances of the Hyades were measured by this method, it was found that they were grouped in the shape of a ball or sphere that is 135 light-years away from us.

## THE DISTANCE OF DOUBLE STARS

The distance of spinning twins can be calculated from their orbits, how bright they look, and the information in the mass-luminosity curve. This is how the calculation is made:

Step 1. Astronomers measure the period of the twins' motion in their orbits (the length of time for a round trip). They then take a guess at their masses, usually counting each as double the mass of the sun. They know their guess may be wrong, but they will find a correction for it later. Now they use the formula described on page 82, connecting the mass, the period, and the distance between the twins. Using the period they have measured and the masses that they have guessed, they calculate the distance between the stars.

Step 2. From Step 1 they know how far apart the twins are. From photographs of the sky they know how far apart the twins look. But how far apart they look depends on how far away they are from us. Astronomers can find this distance by fitting the actual separation of the stars across the angle between their direction lines in a diagram like

## *MEASURING DISTANCE WITH A TEST LIGHT*

Suppose a spaceship could fly from the earth to any star in space. If it had a bright taillight, we could watch the progress of the ship by sighting its taillight in our telescopes. The farther the space ship went, the dimmer the taillight would look. When the spaceship pulled up alongside a star, the taillight could serve as a test light for measuring the distance of the star. If we knew how bright the taillight really was, we could figure out how far away it must be to look so dim.

We don't have any spaceships that fly out to the stars. But we do have test lights scattered about in space. The stars themselves can serve as test lights if we can find out how bright they really are.

## *THE BLINKING YARDSTICK*

There are many Cepheid variable stars scattered through space. They became important test lights when the astronomers discovered a way of recognizing their real brightness.

In the sky of the southern hemisphere there are the two cloudlike patches of light known as the *Magellanic Clouds* named after the explorer Magellan. Each Cloud is made up of hundreds of thousands of stars that look very faint because the Clouds are very far away. In each Cloud there are hundreds of Cepheid variables. From photographs of the Clouds, the astronomers measured the apparent brightness of these blinking stars. They measured the average brightness of each star, and the rhythm with which it blinks. Then they compared the Cepheids that were together in one Cloud.

First the astronomers found that some Cepheids looked brighter than others in the same Cloud. Now, when one star looks brighter than another, it might be because it is nearer to us, or it might be because its real brightness is greater. But the Cepheids that are neighbors in one Cloud are all about the same distance from us. So they differ in apparent brightness only because they differ in real brightness. When one of them looks ten times as bright as another, it really is ten times as bright.

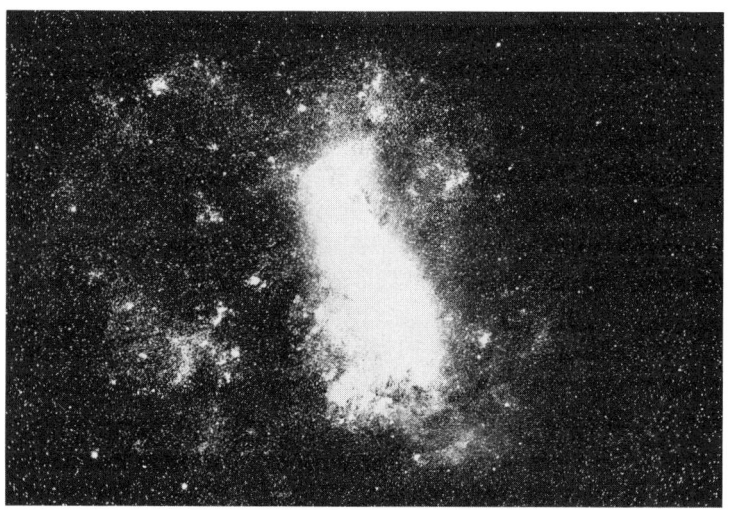

The Large Magellanic Cloud. The study of blinking stars in this galaxy led to the discovery of a yardstick for measuring how far away it is. YERKES OBSERVATORY

The Cepheids in the same Cloud also blinked with different rhythms. Some took only a day to go through a complete cycle of changes in brightness. Others took as much as fifty days. A comparison of the rhythms and brightness led to an important discovery. The brighter a

Cepheid star is, the more time it takes for its blinking. This rule is shown in the following chart. In this chart, each dot stands for a Cepheid star in one of the Magellanic Clouds. The stars are arranged from left to right in the order of the length of their periods. The stars with the shortest periods are at the left, and the stars with the longest periods are at the right. At the same time they are arranged from

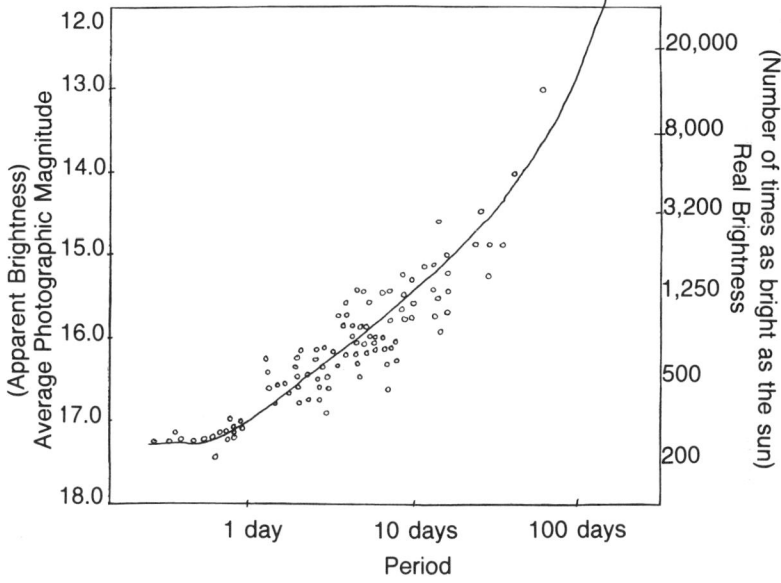

ORIGINAL PERIOD LUMINOSITY CURVE

bottom to top in the order of their brightness. Those that are faintest are at the bottom. The brightest stars are at the top. Notice how they all cluster around the line that goes from the lower left-hand corner to the upper right-hand corner of the chart. This line is know as the *period-luminosity curve* for Cepheid variables.

At first the chart showed only the periods (the numbers at the bottom of the chart), and the apparent brightness of the Cepheids in the Cloud (the numbers at the left of the chart). The chart arranged the stars in the order of their real brightness but didn't tell what the real brightness was. If the astronomers could only find out the *average* real brightness of the Cepheids, the chart would tell the real brightness of any one of them by showing how much fainter or brighter it is than the average. To get this information, the astronomers turned their attention to Cepheids that are not in the Magellanic Clouds. There are Cepheids that are much closer to us than those in the Clouds. If we knew how far away they were, we could figure out their real brightness from their apparent brightness. The astronomers found that they couldn't measure the distance of any *one* of them, because they weren't near enough. But they could measure the average distance of a *group* of them. As the sun moves along among the stars, the stars stream past it in the opposite direction. Those that are nearer the sun stream by more quickly. Those that are farther away stream by more slowly. By measuring the average speed with which a group of Cepheids streams by, the astronomers found their average distance. From this they calculated their average real brightness. This was the key they needed to find the real brightness of every Cepheid. They knew the short-period stars were fainter than the average, and the longer-period stars were brighter than the average. The real brightnesses they calculated are shown by the numbers on the right-hand side of the chart.

Now that we have the complete period-luminosity chart, every Cepheid serves as a test light. Its blinking light gives us a yardstick for measuring how far away it is. First we measure the number of days in the period of the star. Then, from the period-luminosity curve, we find out the real brightness of a star that has that period. From the real brightness we figure out how far away it must be to look as dim as it does. If the Cepheid is one of a group of stars that are together in space, then the distance of the Cepheid tells us the distance of the whole group. This is how the astronomers found out the distances of the Magellanic Clouds. The Clouds are about 200,000 light-years away.

## THE COLOR OF THE STARS

In the spectrum of a star, the colors in its light are spread out side by side. Dark lines in the spectrum show which colors were pulled out of the light by the chemicals on the surface of the star. Some stars have spectra that look alike. But there are many different kinds of spectra. Lines that show up in the spectra of some stars are missing in the spectra of others. Lines that are strong and dark in the spectra of some stars may be weak or faint in the spectra of others. After studying the spectra of many stars, the astronomers found that they could arrange the different kinds of spectra one under the other, so that spectra placed next to each other were almost the same. In this arrangement, as you look from one spectrum to the next, you see a gradual change in the dark lines of the spectrum. As you run your eye from the spectrum on top to the spectrum on the bottom, you see some lines fade out while others appear and grow darker. You also see that the stars are arranged in this way by their color, with blue stars at one end and red stars at the other. This arrangement has been divided into groups or classes, and each class of spectra has been given a letter of the alphabet as its name. The names are in this order: *O, B, A, F, G, K, M, R, N, S.* Stars in classes *O* and *B* are bluish-white, like most of the stars in the constellation Orion. Stars in class *A* are white, like Sirius and Vega. Stars in class *G* are yellow, like Capella and the sun. Stars in class *K* are orange, like Arcturus. Stars in class *M* are red, like Antares. Classes *R, N,* and *S* are also red.

## MEASURING DISTANCE BY COLOR

Every time the astronomers measured the distance of a star, they learned its real brightness too. After measuring the distances of many stars, they compared their real

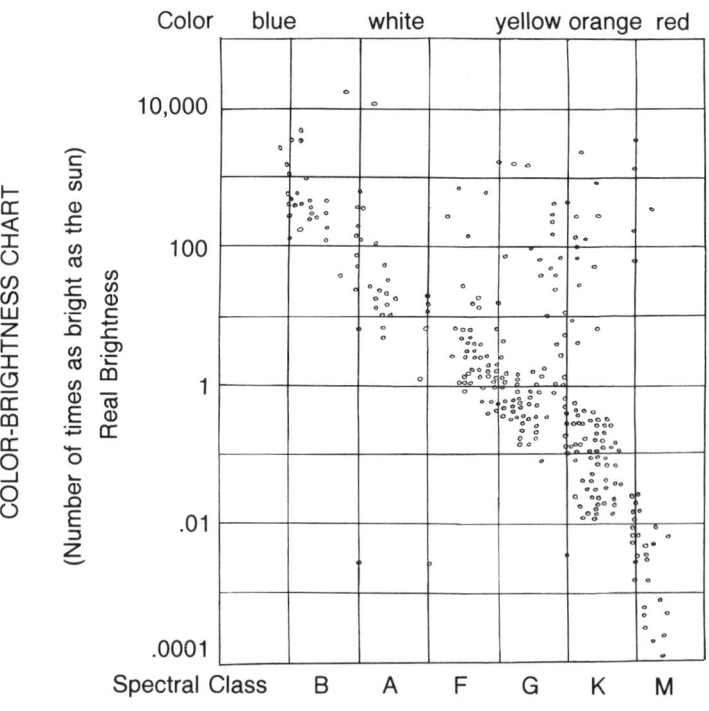

brightness and their color or spectral class. This led to a remarkable discovery. *You can recognize the real brightness of a star by the kind of spectrum that it has.* The connection between real brightness and spectrum is shown in the color-brightness chart. Each dot represents a star whose distance and real brightness had been measured. The stars are arranged from left to right in the order of their color or spectral class. The blue stars are at the left, and the red stars are at the right. At the same time, they are arranged from bottom to top in order of brightness. The faintest stars are at the bottom, and the brightest stars are at the top. Notice that most of the stars cluster along a line that runs from the upper left-hand corner to the lower right-hand corner. This line shows that, for most stars, the redder a star is, the fainter it is. Stars along this line are called stars of the *main sequence.* But there are enough exceptions to spoil the rule. The scattered dots above and below this line represent stars that are brighter or fainter than stars in the main sequence. The brightest stars are called *giants.* The faintest stars are called *dwarfs.* While most white stars are bright, there are some white stars that are faint. While most red stars are faint, there are some red stars that are bright. So the color of a star, by itself, does not tell us how bright the star is. But there is another clue in the spectra of the stars. The spectra of stars of the same color or class are almost the same, but not quite. There are some lines that are dark in the giants, but faint in the dwarfs. Other lines are faint in the giants, and dark in the dwarfs. So you can recognize the brightness of a star of any color by the darkness or faintness of such lines in its spectrum.

Now suppose you study the spectrum of a star whose

distance has never been measured before. By its color and the lines in its spectrum you find out what spectral class it belongs to. Then, by comparing the lines of its spectrum with the lines of giants and dwarfs in that class, you find out how bright it is. But once you know its real brightness, the star becomes a test light. You can figure out its distance by comparing how bright it is with how bright it looks.

## TWO TYPES OF STARS

The Great Nebula in Andromeda is a very distant group of stars. Only the brightest stars in it show up as separate spots on a photograph. The rest combine their

The Great Nebula in Andromeda. This is a galaxy of stars like the Milky Way. The light from this galaxy takes two million years to reach us. YERKES OBSERVATORY

light into a big bright smear. The first separate stars that were seen were bluish-white giants. They were found only in the spiral arms of the galaxy. The astronomers looked for separate stars in the bright center of the nebula, but could not find any that were bright enough to be seen. They tried again in 1941, using new photographic plates that are sensitive to red light. This time they found separate stars in the center. They were all red giants. They hadn't been seen before because the old-type photographic plates couldn't "see" red.

Seeing the red giants in the Great Nebula in Andromeda was the first step in an important discovery: There are two different types of stars. One type, now called *population I,* is found only in dusty places like the spiral arms. The other type, called *population II,* is found in the

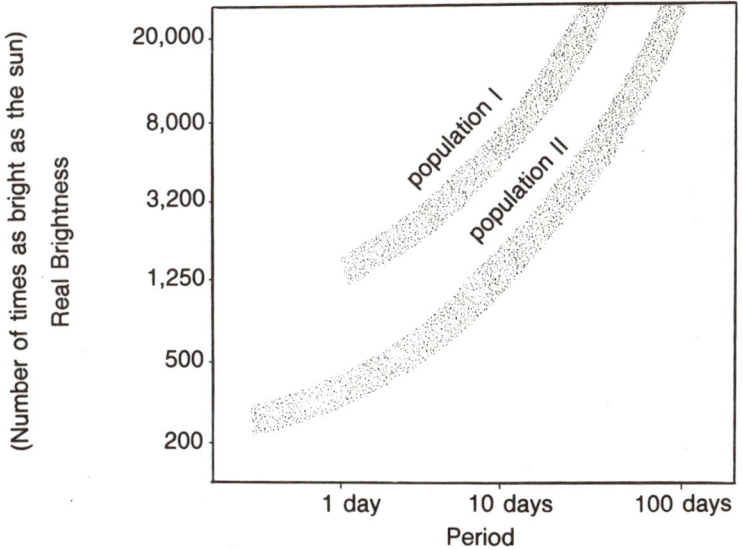

NEW PERIOD-LUMINOSITY CURVES

center of the Galaxy and between the spiral arms, where there is no dust or gas. The Milky Way galaxy is divided into two populations in the same way. The sun is in a spiral arm of the Galaxy, so the sun and its neighbors belong to population I. The stars in globular clusters are not surrounded by dust and gas. They belong to population II.

This discovery helped to wipe out an important mistake the astronomers had made. They used to think that all Cepheid variables fit into one period-luminosity curve. Now they found out that Cepheids in population I are about 1½ magnitudes brighter than Cepheids of the same period in population II. So they really need two curves, one for each population. When they first calculated the distance of the Great Nebula in Andromeda, they had used the wrong curve for the Cepheids in the spiral arms. It led them to believe that the Nebula was one million light-years away. By using the right curve now, they found that the Nebula was really twice as far away as they thought.

## *TEST LIGHTS FOR GREAT DISTANCES*

The farther away a star is, the less of its light we get. If the star is very far away, we may not get enough of its light to make a clear spectrum. In that case, we cannot use its spectrum to measure its distance.

The most distant stars are seen grouped together in cloudlike crowds called the galaxies. To measure how far away a galaxy is, all we have to do is find one or more stars in the crowd that can serve as test lights. We have already seen how the Cepheid variables serve as test lights. Other good test lights are stars of spectral class *B,* and novae.

The stars of class *B* are among the brightest, so, at a great distance, they are more easily seen than other fainter stars. The color-brightness chart shows that stars of class *B* all have about the same real brightness. Assuming that class *B* stars that are far away have the same real brightness as those represented in the chart, we can figure out how far away they are from how faint they look.

Novae appear from time to time in the distant crowds of stars. When they flare up, novae do not all become equally bright. But the average of many novae is pretty nearly always the same. Assuming that novae that are very far away have the same average brightness as those that are closest to us, we can figure out how far away they are by how faint they look.

Today, separate stars can serve as test lights only for a distance of about 30 million light-years. Galaxies that are beyond that distance show up on photographs only as blurs of light. Even the 200-inch telescope on Mt. Palomar, the largest telescope in the United States, is not powerful enough to show separate stars in these galaxies. To measure their distances, another test light is needed. The test light that is used is the galaxy itself. There are hundreds of galaxies less than 20 million light-years away. From their apparent brightnesses and their distances the astronomers can calculate their real brightness. The average galaxy is as bright as 10,000 million suns. Assuming that the more distant galaxies have the same average real brightness, we can estimate *their* distances by how faint they look.

# 9 Giants and Dwarfs

## ☆ TAKING A STAR'S TEMPERATURE

If you heat a piece of iron until it glows, first it becomes *red*-hot. Then, as the temperature rises higher, the glowing iron changes color until it becomes *white*-hot. This shows that the temperature of a hot glowing body is related to the color of the light it sends out. Because of this, we can judge the temperature at the surface of a star by its color. The red stars are the coolest. The bluish-white stars are the hottest.

To get a measure for the temperature, we first need a measure for the color of a star. The color index described in Chapter 4 is such a measure. The color index is the difference between how bright a star looks to the eye and how bright it looks to an ordinary photographic plate. Because the eye is sensitive to red light while a photographic plate is not, this difference shows what part of the light is red. So the color index is a measure of how much or how little of the light of a star is red.

By studying glowing bodies in the laboratory, physicists discovered a formula by which they can calculate the temperature of a body from its color index. They use this formula to figure out the temperature at the surface of a star. A red star like Antares has a surface temperature of about 2,800 degrees Celsius, or 5,100 degrees Fahrenheit. An orange star like Arcturus has a temperature of 3,800 degrees Celsius, or 6,900 degrees Fahrenheit. Capella, a yellow star, has a temperature of 5,300 degrees Celsius, or 9,500 degrees Fahrenheit. Sirius, a white star, has a temperature of 11,000 degrees Celsius, or 19,700 degrees Fahrenheit.

The temperature of a star can also be calculated from its heat index, described in Chapter 4.

## *THE DARK-LINE THERMOMETER*

The dark lines in the spectrum of a star are the fingerprints of the chemicals that are on the surface of the star. Each chemical element puts certain special lines into the spectrum. This was found out by studying the spectra of hot gases in the laboratory. When these studies were made, another important fact was discovered. The lines that a chemical puts into the spectrum depend on the temperature of the gas. So the lines we find in the spectrum of a star tell us two things. They tell us what chemical elements there are in the gas at the surface of the star. They also tell us the temperature of the gas. The dark lines in the spectrum give us another thermometer for measuring the temperature of a star.

By using different ways of measuring the temperature of a star, the astronomers check and double check their results.

## GAS AND DUST IN SPACE

There are dust and gas in the space between the stars. This was proved by studying the dark patches that are found in the Milky Way. They turned out to be large dark clouds in space that block the light of the stars behind them. It is also proved by many other facts. Photographs of a supernova show gas, blown out by the explosion, rushing away from the star in all directions. Some other stars, too, are surrounded by glowing clouds of gas. The earth is bombarded every day by small particles called *cosmic rays* that crash in at high speed from outer space. All these facts show that "empty" space isn't empty at all.

## TROUBLE FOR ASTRONOMERS

The fact that there is dust in the space between the stars means trouble for the astronomers. Dust interferes with the passage of light from a star to us. It blocks and scatters some of the light. This makes every star look dimmer than it would if there were no dust in space. Since we judge the star's distance, mass, and size by its brightness, dust makes all these calculations wrong. Dust is also choosy about which light it scatters. It scatters blue light and lets the red light go through. So dust makes stars look redder than they really are. But we calculate the temperature of a star from its color. So dust makes this calculation wrong, too. Dust gives the astronomers a nice riddle to solve: How do you get correct calculations from wrong information?

## SOLVING THE RIDDLE

The astronomers have solved so many difficult riddles, we are not surprised that they solved this one too. They found a way of measuring how much dust there is in space. Then they could tell how much starlight the dust scatters. With this information they could correct the errors the dust introduced into their calculations.

A clue to the amount of dust between us and a star is in one of the errors it forces us to make. One way of measuring the temperature of a star is by its color. This measure comes out wrong because the dust makes the star look redder than it is. Another way of measuring the temperature of a star is by recognizing the dark lines in its spectrum. This measure comes out *right,* because the dust does not disturb the position of the lines. By using the right temperature (judged from the lines in the spectrum), astronomers can find out what the true color of the star is. By comparing the true color with the color they see, they can figure out how much light was scattered by the dust. From this information they can figure out how much dust did the scattering. Calculations like this tell them where the dust is thick and where it is thin. On the average, there is enough dust in space to make a star look one magnitude dimmer than it should for every thousand parsecs that its light travels through space.

## *COLOR AND BRIGHTNESS*

When a piece of iron is heated, first it gives off a faint red glow. As it gets hotter, its color changes. At the same time it becomes brighter and brighter. A white-hot iron is brighter than a red-hot iron. This shows that when a hot object glows, its brightness is related to its color. For this reason, the real brightness of a star depends partly on its color. If two stars are the same size, and one is white while the other is red, the white star is brighter than the red star.

## SIZE AND BRIGHTNESS

But brightness is also related to size. Suppose we heat a lot of flat square plates, each one inch wide, until they are white-hot at the same temperature. The face of one of these squares alone sends out a certain amount of light. This amount can be calculated from its temperature. Two

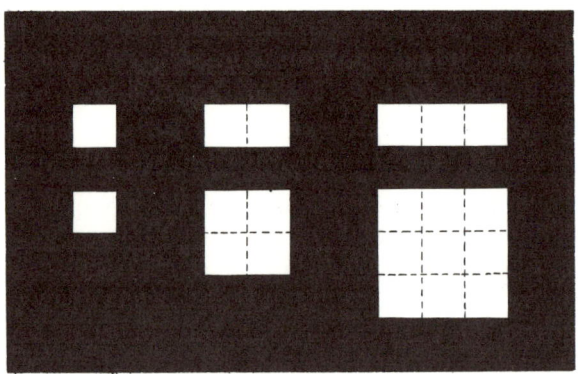

squares lying side by side would send out twice as much light. Three squares would send out three times as much light. We can make a square two inches wide by using four of the small squares. So a square two inches wide would send out four times as much light as a square one inch wide. A three-inch square would be nine times as bright as a one-inch square. The brightness of a glowing plate depends on how many square inches there are in its face.

The brightness of a star is related to its size in the same way. Every square inch of its surface sends out a fixed amount of light that depends on its temperature and color. So the brightness of the star depends on how many square inches there are in its surface. Since a larger star has a wider surface, the larger a star is, the brighter it is, compared to other stars of the same color. Its brightness depends on its width in the same way that it did in the case of the square plates. If one star is twice as wide as another of the same color, it is four times as bright. If it is three times as wide, it is nine times as bright.

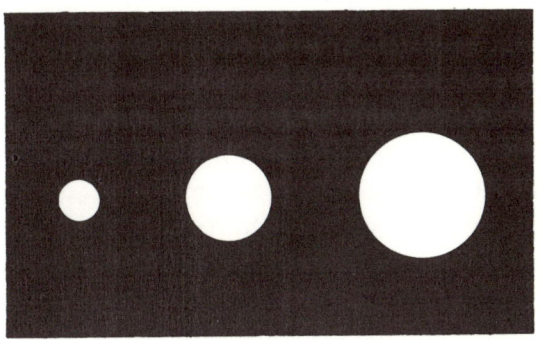

## HOW LARGE ARE THE STARS?

Because brightness depends on size as well as color, we can calculate the size of a star from its color and its real brightness. A square inch of a certain color sends out a definite amount of light. This amount can be calculated from the color or temperature. But when we know how much light one square inch of a star sends out, we can figure out how many square inches it must have in its face to send out as much light as it does. And when we know the area of its face, we can figure out how wide it is. This is done with the help of a formula learned in geometry.

## RED GIANTS AND WHITE DWARFS

A square inch of the surface of a star sends out an

amount of light that depends on its color. This amount is very small if the star is red. It is high if the star is white. Since every square inch of a red star has only a faint glow, the star as a whole can be very bright only if it has very many square inches of surface. So a bright red star must be very big, and is called a *red giant*. Since every square inch of a white star has a bright glow, the star as a whole can be very faint only if it has very few square inches of surface. So a faint white star must be very small, and is called a *white dwarf*. The red giants are the largest stars. The white dwarfs are among the smallest. (Neutron stars, described later, are smaller than white dwarfs.)

Antares is a red giant. Its width, calculated from its color and real brightness, is 400 million miles. This is about twice the width of the orbit the earth follows around the sun. If Antares were placed where the sun is, the earth would be inside the star, halfway between the center and the surface.

The first white dwarf that was discovered is the little companion of Sirius that revolves around it once every fifty years. Its width, calculated from its color and real brightness, is only twenty-nine thousand miles. The earth is eight thousand miles wide. So the companion of Sirius is only about three times as wide as the earth. Another white dwarf, known as Van Maanen's star, is six thousand miles wide, so it is actually smaller than the earth.

## *CHECKING THE WIDTH*

We said that the stars are so far away that when we look at them we see no size at all. This is not strictly true. Our eyes and our photographic plates cannot detect the size of the stars, but there is an instrument that can. It is called the *interferometer*. With this instrument it is possible to measure the width of some of the larger stars directly. The farther away a star is, the smaller it looks. The interferometer tells us how wide it looks. Then, if we know how far away the star is, we can figure out how wide it really is. The widths measured by the interferometer agree with those calculated from the real brightness and color of the stars. This proves that the color-brightness method of measuring the width of a star is reliable.

## *THE DENSITY OF THE STARS*

The particles in a gas may be packed close together, or they may be spread out thinly in space. The more the particles are crowded together, the heavier each cubic inch of the gas will be. The mass of one cubic inch of a gas is called its *density*.

In Chapter 7 we found out how the astronomers measure the mass of a star. In this chapter we have seen how they measure the width of a star. When you know the width of a star, you can figure out how many cubic inches it contains by using a formula learned in geometry. Then you can find the density of the star by dividing the mass by the number of cubic inches in its volume. A star crowded into a small volume has a very high density. A star spread out in a very big volume has a low density. The smallest stars, the white dwarfs and the neutron stars, are the densest. The largest stars, the red giants, are the least dense. The white dwarf that revolves around Sirius is so dense that one cubic inch of it weighs one ton. But even this is thin compared to what is packed into a neutron star.

A neutron star is so dense that a cubic inch of it weighs about 1,000 million tons! On the other hand, the red giant Antares is spread out so thinly that the air we breathe is three thousand times as dense as Antares is.

# 10 New Windows on the Stars

## ☆ ASTRONOMY'S PARTNERS

Astronomers do not work alone when they study the stars. They have help from industry and from other scientists. Industry helps by inventing and producing tools that the astronomer can use. Other scientists help by supplying facts obtained through laboratory experiments and theories that tie the facts together and explain them. The astronomer uses these facts and theories to draw conclusions from the coded messages that come from the stars. In the earlier chapters of this book we have seen examples of this help. The invention of the telescope, the spectroscope, and the camera gave the astronomer tools for catching and concentrating starlight, spreading it out as a spectrum, and recording it as a picture. Other tools helped to make measurements on these photographs. Then, using such branches of science as the theories of motion, heat, light, and atomic structure, the astronomer could figure out from these measurements how far away a star is, how hot it is, how heavy it is, how it moves, and even what chemical elements are on its surface.

There have been great changes in science and industry since World War II. A new branch of science, *particle physics,* has grown up, providing information on the behavior of the particles that are inside the atomic nucleus. A new industry, the electronics industry, which had already produced radio transmitters and receivers, has created such new tools as television cameras and picture tubes, particle detectors, and high-speed computers. In addition, the space programs organized by several governments have produced rockets that can rise above the earth's atmosphere, man-made earth satellites, and spaceships that travel to the moon and back. These advances of science and industry have given astronomers new and improved ways of studying the stars.

## AIDS FOR THE TELESCOPE

Before the telescope was invented, the astronomer's eye was the detector that received the light of the star being observed. When the telescope was first invented, the eye continued to be the detector. The job of the telescope was to catch the light over an area wider than the eye and then concentrate it in the eye. Concentrating the light made it possible to detect the feebler light coming from more distant stars. After the camera was invented, a new detector, the photographic plate, took the place of the eye. Now other more sensitive electronic detectors, such as image intensifiers and television cameras, are used. In these new detectors a small amount of light triggers an avalanche of electric current, turning a weak signal into a stronger signal that can be measured and recorded on a photographic plate. Electronic computers help, too, by setting the telescope more accurately, controlling the measurements made from photographic plates, and making calculations. With all these electronic aids a telescope can see farther into space than it was able to without them.

## NEW TOOLS OPEN NEW WINDOWS

For hundreds of years the astronomer had only one source of information about the stars—the light that comes from them. Recent advances in science and industry have opened up new windows through which other signals from the stars may be received.

The National Radio Astronomy Observatory's 140-foot radio telescope NATIONAL RADIO ASTRONOMY OBSERVATORY

The stars and galaxies are like radio-broadcasting stations. They send out radio signals that pass through the earth's atmosphere and reach the ground. These radio signals cannot be detected with an ordinary telescope, but they can be detected by a radio telescope which is like a radio antenna. The radio telescope gives astronomers the radio window through which they may study stars and galaxies and the space between them.

Stars send out other signals, too, besides light waves and radio waves. These include gamma rays, X rays and ultraviolet rays, whose wavelengths are shorter than the wavelengths of visible light, and infrared rays, whose wavelengths are longer than the wavelengths of visible light. The atmosphere of the earth blocks and scatters the short-wave rays, and smothers the infrared rays by adding to them rays that come from the earth. As a result, the messages carried by these rays either never reach the earth or are thoroughly confused by the time they do. The best way to get these messages before they are scattered or muddied by the atmosphere is to catch them above the atmosphere. This is now possible because rockets, earth satellites, and spaceships can place telescopes and other detectors outside the atmosphere. Earth satellites equipped as flying laboratories have opened up a gamma-ray window, an X-ray window, an ultraviolet window, and an infrared window looking out on the stars.

Gamma rays, X rays, ultraviolet rays, infrared rays, and radio waves are all electric and magnetic vibrations, just as visible light is. Each is an example of what is called radiation, which is a stream of particles of energy called *photons.* Each is a bundle of rays of different wavelengths and frequencies which can be spread out side by side in a spectrum. Each spectrum, like a spectrum of visible light, is a carrier of information: the wavelengths in it are clues to the temperature of the region of space from which the bundle of rays came. Particular lines in it may be recognized as "fingerprints" of nuclei or atoms, or molecules, or physical processes in that region. A Doppler shift of these lines is a clue to the speed with which the matter in this region is moving toward or away from us.

There are two more windows also opened up in recent times. One is a window into the interior of stars, provided by theories that permit astronomers to figure out what is going on inside a star from the signals that come out of it. The other is a window into the past, provided by theories that permit them to figure out how stars change, and how they must have been in the past to change into what they are now.

All these new windows on the stars, and the information they bring us, are discussed in this chapter and in Chapter 11. We shall see that the new information has supplied answers to some old questions but has also raised some new and puzzling ones.

## *THE ATOMS IN THE STARS*

The dark lines in the spectra of the stars show that the chemical elements in the stars are the same as those we find on the earth. There are about one hundred elements in all. The lightest one is hydrogen, and the heaviest one found in nature is uranium. On the earth, each atom of an element is made up of a nucleus surrounded by a cloud of electrons.

The nucleus has a positive electrical charge. The surrounding cloud of electrons has a negative electrical charge. Each nucleus contains two kinds of smaller particles called *protons* and *neutrons*. A proton has a positive electrical charge, and a neutron has no electrical charge. These particles in an atomic nucleus are held together by a force of attraction between them. The cloud of electrons surrounding an atomic nucleus contains as many electrons as there are protons in the nucleus.

A hydrogen nucleus has only one proton in it and only one electron revolving around it. A uranium nucleus contains ninety-two protons and is surrounded by ninety-two electrons. In a cool gas, each nucleus holds on to its electrons, and the whole atom (the nucleus surrounded by its electrons) counts as one particle in the gas. But things are different at the center of a star. Because of the high temperature there, the nucleus can't hold on to its electrons. The electrons are free to wander around. So, at the center of a star, each electron, as well as each nucleus, counts as a separate particle. A hydrogen atom contributes two particles (the nucleus and one electron). A uranium atom contributes ninety-three particles (the nucleus and ninety-two electrons).

To measure the weight of an atom, scientists use the weight of the lightest hydrogen atom as a unit. In this system of measure, the lightest hydrogen atom has a weight of 1. So when a hydrogen atom separates into 2 particles at the center of a star, the average weight of these particles is 1 divided by 2, or ½. The heaviest uranium atom has a weight of 238. So when a uranium atom separates into 93 particles, the average weight of these particles is 238 divided by 93, or about 2½. If all of a star were made of hydrogen, the average weight of its particles would be ½. If all of a star were made of uranium, the average weight of its particles would be about 2½. If a star is a mixture of different elements, the average weight of its particles is between ½ and 2½. The more hydrogen there is in the star, the lower the average weight of the particles is.

When the mass-luminosity curve was discovered, the astronomers worked out a mathematical formula that explained why heavier stars give out more light. This formula showed that the amount of light a star sends out depends on its mass, its width, and the average weight of the particles in it. So when astronomers know the mass, the width, and the real brightness of a star, they can figure out from the formula the average weight of the particles in the star. But from this result they can tell how much of the star is made up of hydrogen. The stars have different amounts of hydrogen in them. Together they have more atoms of hydrogen than of any other element.

## *THE RAW MATERIAL AND FUEL OF THE STARS*

We shall see that radio waves and ultraviolet rays from space show that the gas clouds between stars, like the stars themselves, are also mostly hydrogen. Laboratory experiments show that hydrogen atoms can be combined to form helium atoms and that, step by step, heavier atoms can be built up from hydrogen and helium. These experiments and theoretical calculations show that the stars are atom factories where heavy atoms are made from light ones. Hydrogen and helium are the raw material out of which stars are made.

When hydrogen or helium atoms combine to form heavier atoms, some of the mass is lost. The lost mass is turned into light and heat that make the stars shine. Besides being the raw material of the stars, hydrogen and helium are also their chief fuels.

## OPENING THE RADIO WINDOW

The radio window on the stars was opened by accident. In 1932 a telephone engineer used a bowl-shaped antenna to search for radio waves that might be causing noises in telephone lines. His antenna detected some waves, but he found that they didn't come from any place on the earth or in the air. They came from space. Since

This galaxy in Centaurus is a source of radio noise. HALE OBSERVATORIES

then astronomers have used radio telescopes of many sizes and shapes to study these radio waves. Some of the waves come from clouds of dust and gas; some come from individual stars; and some come from galaxies.

## SEEING THROUGH DUST CLOUDS

When astronomers studied only the visible light coming from stars, they could not see the center of our Galaxy because it is hidden behind big clouds of dust in space. Now they can "see" the center with their radio telescopes, since radio waves pass right through the dust clouds. The radio waves from the core of the Galaxy show that there was a great explosion there about a million years ago.

## CLOUDS OF ATOMS AND MOLECULES

The clouds of gas and dust in the Galaxy are also sending out radio waves. These waves come from hydrogen atoms and from over thirty-nine different kinds of molecules that are like little broadcasting stations. Their broadcasts come to us without words. They give the astronomers information from which they have made a detailed map of the Galaxy and have shown that it is spinning like a top. The map gives additional proof that the Galaxy has three spiral arms, which are the dustiest part of the Galaxy.

## STARS THAT EXPLODED

The radio waves from some gas clouds in the Galaxy show that the clouds are expanding very rapidly, with the outer edge of each cloud rushing away from its center at great speed. This is proof that a star at the center of the cloud exploded a long time ago and threw out the cloud of gas. From the size of the cloud and the speed at which its outer edge is moving, it is possible to figure out when the explosion took place.

In 1968 radio pulses were detected for the first time coming from the centers of such explosions. The radio waves are produced by a small, dense, rapidly spinning star that is all that is left of the star that exploded. Because it pulses, it is called a *pulsar*. In some of these remnants of explosions, the temperature was high enough to force the electrons into the protons inside the atomic nuclei. When an electron is forced into a proton, they combine to form a neutron. The nuclei disintegrate, and what is left is a neutron gas packed into a smaller space. Stars like these are called *neutron stars.*

Pulsars are only one of many kinds of stars that send out radio waves. Others that have been detected by their radio waves are red-dwarf flare stars, red supergiants, and a blue-dwarf companion to a red supergiant.

## *EXPLODING GALAXIES*

Some radio waves have been found to come from exploding galaxies. Each such galaxy has a magnetic field similar to that of a bar magnet. A magnetic field tends to push any magnetic pole or charged particle that enters it. Scientists picture a field as a collection of lines called *lines of force*. A magnetic pole in a magnetic field moves along a line of force. A charged particle spirals around a line of force. The explosion of a galaxy throws out charged particles. Each particle, as it spirals around a line of force in the magnetic field, sends out radio waves. These waves are called *synchrotron radiation* because radiation produced in this way was first observed in the laboratory in particle accelerators called *synchrotrons,* used to make charged particles move faster and faster.

## THE EXPLOSION THAT STARTED IT ALL

We have seen that the galaxies are moving away from us, and that the farther away they are, the faster they move away. Scientists assume that the way the universe looks from the earth is no different from the way it would look from any other part of the universe. On this assumption, the galaxies seen from any place in the universe would seem to be moving away from that place, with the more distant galaxies moving faster. This would be possible only if all galaxies were moving away from each other, with the spaces between them growing steadily larger. This is the theory of the *Expanding Universe.* The whole universe is expanding as if it had all been packed into a small space sometime in the past and then an explosion made it fly apart. This explosion that is assumed to have started the expansion of the universe is sometimes referred to as the *Big Bang.* Radio astronomy has produced two important pieces of evidence that support the theory that the Big Bang actually took place. (1) The theory of the Big Bang predicts that the universe, at the time it exploded, contained a lot of radiation at a high temperature, and that the expansion of the universe cooled the radiation down to a temperature of about 3 degrees Kelvin (about 270 degrees below zero Celsius). At this temperature the radiation left over from the Big Bang, after having had its wavelength lengthened by the Doppler shift caused by the expansion, would consist of radio waves. These radio waves have been detected and they do fit a temperature of 3 degrees Kelvin. (2) Radio waves show that some of the hydrogen in space is the heavy hydrogen known as *deuterium*. This supports the theory of the Big Bang because calculations show that only the Big Bang could have produced the deuterium that has been found. The nuclear processes in stars could not have produced the deuterium because, although they do make some, they use up more than they make.

## *FLYING OBSERVATORIES*

Since the first Russian Sputnik opened up the space age in 1957, many American earth satellites have been put into orbit. Some of them are equipped as astronomical

Orbiting Astronomical Observatory in earth orbit NASA

observatories. The satellite called OAO-II (Orbiting Astronomical Observatory-II) was successfully launched in 1968 (after an earlier failure with OAO-I) with special equipment for receiving and measuring ultraviolet rays from space and the stars. In 1970 the satellite called UHURU was launched, equipped with detectors designed to receive X rays. This satellite, and others that followed it, extended the first X-ray studies that began in 1962 with rocket probes of the upper atmosphere.

In 1963 the United States and the Soviet Union signed a treaty in which they agreed not to explode nuclear devices in the atmosphere or in space. To check on whether the agreement is being kept, the United States has, since 1963, launched a series of Vela satellites equipped with instruments that would detect the gamma rays released by a nuclear explosion. The same equipment can also detect gamma rays coming from stars.

Another series of earth satellites called OSO (Orbiting Solar Observatory) has been put into orbit to study the sun. Balloons have been sent up to study infrared rays. The Apollo spaceships went to the moon to study the moon and space as seen from the moon.

## *THE ULTRAVIOLET WINDOW*

The rays of sunlight and starlight that enter the earth's atmosphere include ultraviolet rays as well as visible light. Most of the ultraviolet rays never reach the ground because they are stopped by the ozone layer that is about fourteen miles above the ground. Since the OAO satellites are in orbits above the ozone layer, they can detect these rays. Each satellite is equipped with telescopes that catch and concentrate the rays, spectrometers that separate them by wavelength, and detectors that measure the amount of energy received in each wavelength. The recorded measurements are transmitted to the ground by radio. The ultraviolet rays detected have come from galaxies, from individual stars, from gas and dust between the stars, from planets, and from comets. The information carried by these rays has led to many new discoveries. One of them is that there are hydrogen molecules in space in addition to the separate hydrogen atoms that had been discovered earlier. Each hydrogen molecule has two atoms in it. In some of these molecules one of the hydrogen atoms is deuterium, the heavy form of hydrogen. The ultraviolet rays detected also showed that there are separate deuterium atoms in space.

## *THE QUASAR PUZZLE*

Some of the ultraviolet light detected by the OAO satellites comes from the very strange things that are now called *quasars,* an abbreviation for quasi-stellar objects. Quasars are bright enough to be seen as stars on photographic plates. Their spectra show that they are moving away from us two or three times as fast as the most distant galaxies. Among galaxies, motion away from us and distance go hand in hand. The faster the motion away from us, the farther away the galaxy is. If this rule applies to the quasars, they are farther away than any known galaxy. On the other hand, we receive strong signals from them in the form of radio waves, ultraviolet rays and infrared rays. If the quasars are really as far away as they seem to be, the signals we receive could be as strong as they are only if a quasar radiates a hundred times as much energy as the whole Milky Way, which has about 100,000 million stars in it. Two questions remain unanswered: Are the quasars really as far away as they seem to be; and if they are, How do they produce such great quantities of energy?

## THE X-RAY WINDOW

The UHURU and OSO satellites have detected X rays coming from galaxies and from quasars. There are also X rays coming from pulsars and from globular clusters. Astronomers think that some X-ray sources may be *black holes*. A black hole is a small, very dense neutron star that weighs at least three times as much as the sun and has a gravitational pull so strong that no light can escape from it. The X rays received from a black hole would come from gas particles trapped in orbit around the black hole. There may be black holes at the centers of globular clusters. There may also be one at the center of the Milky Way.

It is possible that the X-ray source called Cygnus X-1 may be a black hole. It is associated with a star that behaves as though it had a companion revolving around it, but the companion is *invisible.* Moreover, the companion is eight times as heavy as the sun, which is heavy enough for it to be a black hole.

## INFRARED WINDOWS

Infrared rays have wavelengths that are longer than those of visible light but shorter than those of radio waves. Most infrared rays that enter the earth's atmosphere are absorbed by the water, carbon dioxide, and ozone in the air. There are some wavelengths, however, that are not absorbed and reach the ground. They provide infrared windows on the stars. Balloons, airplanes, and satellites have opened up other windows using the wavelengths that never reach the ground.

Infrared rays are found to come from many different sources in space. Some come from shells of dust surrounding stars. The dust catches some of the starlight and is made warm enough to radiate infrared rays. There is also a large amount of infrared energy coming from the center of the Galaxy.

Through infrared rays, astronomers may have detected stars that are just being born. Some infrared rays come from large gas clouds that are probably beginning to contract to form a star. The contraction has made them warm enough to send out infrared rays but not yet warm enough to send out visible light.

## *THE GAMMA-RAY WINDOW*

Since 1963 the Vela satellites have been searching the sky for gamma rays to be sure that the treaty banning nuclear explosions in the atmosphere or in space is not being violated. In 1967 some gamma rays were detected, but no violation of the treaty had taken place. The gamma rays came from outside the solar system. Since then astronomers have made a systematic study of gamma-ray bursts that come from outer space. Many theories have been constructed that might explain what produces them, but none of the theories has yet been proved. So far, then, the gamma-ray window is an opening to a great mystery.

## *THE TELESCOPE IN A GOLD MINE*

When astronomers look at the sun through a telescope, they see its surface, not its interior. They have seen its interior only with their "mind's eyes" through theoretical calculations. Using knowledge obtained through laboratory experiments, they have figured out what kind of processes there might be in the sun that could produce the energy that is coming out of it. The theoretical picture that they have drawn is that deep inside the sun hydrogen nuclei are combining to form helium nuclei, and releasing energy and small, electrically neutral particles called *neutrinos* at the same time. To check whether this picture is right, they have constructed a special kind of "telescope" capable of catching neutrinos and counting them. The "telescope" is a big tank of cleaning fluid in a gold mine that is one mile underground. It was set up in a mine because the mile-thick layer of rock above it was needed to prevent cosmic rays from entering the tank and confusing the experiment. While cosmic rays cannot pass through a mile-thick layer of rock, neutrinos can do so easily because they are very small, have no electric charge, and are weightless. It was expected that some of the neutrinos that enter the tank would collide with chlorine atoms in the cleaning fluid and change them to argon atoms. Then the argon atoms could be removed and counted. Theoretical calculations predicted that on the average one argon atom would be produced per day. After conducting the experiment for many months, the scientists found that the number of argon atoms produced was lower than expected. This has left them with a puzzle to solve: Is the picture they had formed of the sun's interior wrong? Does the sun really produce as many neutrinos as they thought it did? If it does, Why don't the right number of them show up in the tank? The experiment is being continued, and more theoretical work is being done to try to solve this puzzle.

# 11 The Evolution of the Stars

☆─────────────────────────

The universe is everything that exists. It extends as far as our telescopes can see, and beyond. By studying the stars and the space between the stars, we have begun to get a picture of the size, shape, and history of the universe.

## A LUMPY UNIVERSE

From the directions in which we see the stars, and their distances from us, we know how they are spread out in space. Although they are scattered far and wide, they are not spread out evenly. We live in a lumpy universe. The stars are found in big groups or galaxies, separated by wide spaces.

## A MOVING PICTURE OF THE UNIVERSE

Astronomers have two sources of information about the universe. One source is the body of facts and theories based on their own observations of stars and galaxies. The other source is the body of facts and theories of physics, based on laboratory experiments to study the behavior of gases, liquids, and solids, energy in all its forms, and the structure of atoms and molecules. By putting together information from these two sources, astronomers have constructed a model of the universe. The model is like a moving picture expressed in the form of mathematical equations. It describes how the universe looks now, and predicts how it will change as time passes.

## REVERSING THE PICTURE

A moving picture can be made to run backward. If the picture on the screen shows a girl diving into a swimming pool, the picture running backward shows the girl jumping out of the pool upside down and landing on her feet on the diving board. The astronomers' moving picture of the universe can be run backward, too, to the time of the Big Bang. Running the picture forward again shows the universe from the beginning, and traces the history of the universe and the evolution of atoms, galaxies, and stars.

## AT THE TIME OF THE BIG BANG

Calculations show that the Big Bang must have taken place about 17,000 million years ago. Before the explosion that started the expansion of the universe, all the matter of the universe was densely packed together. The universe was not lumpy; instead, there was a uniform mixture of matter and radiation everywhere. The temperature was about 1,000,000 million degrees Kelvin. At that temperature no atoms could exist. There were only photons of radiation, and elementary particles of matter such as protons, neutrons, electrons, positrons (which are like electrons, except that they have a positive charge), neutrinos, and antineutrinos. There was a constant interchange between the radiation and matter. Some gamma-ray photons split to form electron-positron pairs, and some of these pairs combined again to form gamma-ray photons. But the balance favored the radiation.

Before the Big Bang the total mass of all the radiation was greater than the total mass of all the particles of matter. After the Big Bang, conditions changed very rapidly at first, then more slowly as time passed. During the first three seconds the temperature dropped to 5,000 million degrees Kelvin. Some of the neutrons split into protons and electrons. During the next three minutes the temperature dropped to 1,000 million degrees. Some neutrons and protons began to combine to form helium nuclei, and perhaps also nuclei of lithium, beryllium, and boron. After a few more minutes the mass that was not stored in radiation was divided in the ratio 3 to 1 between hydrogen nuclei (protons) and helium nuclei (each with two protons and two neutrons). There were also enough electrons to balance the electrical charges of the protons.

## *THE BIRTH OF GLOBULAR CLUSTERS AND GALAXIES*

As time passed, the amount of mass stored in radiation decreased, and the amount of mass in matter increased. About 1,000 million years after the Big Bang, the amount of mass was evenly divided between the two. After that, there was more mass stored in matter than in radiation.

Meanwhile clouds of hydrogen and helium nuclei, accompanied by electrons, were swirling around in space.

Their motion was made up of two parts: the outward motion that resulted from the Big Bang, and the disordered motion of the individual particles darting about in all directions. The disordered motion sometimes crowded more particles into one place than another, so some lumpiness began to appear in the universe in the form of separated clouds of particles. At first these separated clouds were

A globular cluster of stars, in the constellation Hercules HALE OBSERVATORIES

only temporary, breaking up again and reforming again as the disorderly motion of the particles concentrated them now here, now there. But finally, when the temperature was low enough, in some clouds that were big enough, the force of gravity that tends to pull the particles together was strong enough to overcome the motion of the particles that tends to pull them apart. Calculations show that the smallest cloud in which this could happen at the temperature that existed then had to have about the mass of a globular cluster, which is about 5 million times the mass of the sun. Stable clouds of this size began to form perhaps as early as 200 million years after the Big Bang. Some of these, drawn to each other by the force of gravity, could have collided to form the larger stable clouds with masses about equal to those of galaxies, namely, hundreds of thousands of millions times the mass of the sun. Later, when the temperature fell low enough, smaller clouds within them with only enough mass to form a star could be separate and stable. Thus the galaxies began to take shape, with stars within them, and globular clusters of stars surrounding them.

## *THE TWO CLASSES OF GALAXIES AND STARS*

The clouds from which globular clusters and the first galaxies were formed contained only gas, and had no spinning motion. Since there was no dust, the stars formed within them were population II stars. Since there was no rotation in the clouds from which they formed, the globular clusters were perfect spheres, and the galaxies were

A spiral galaxy in Canes Venatici HALE OBSERVATORIES

elliptical. In some stars, as we shall see below, atoms heavier than helium were being formed. When the stars grew old and exploded, they spewed the heavy atoms into space, where they condensed into dust. The outward motion of the explosions gradually introduced spinning motion in the dusty clouds. The spinning dusty clouds later became flattened, spinning spiral galaxies. The stars formed in the spiral arms, fed by dust as well as gas when they were born, were population I stars.

Population I stars are said to be "metal rich" because about 2 percent of their mass consists of atomic nuclei that are heavier than helium. Population II stars are "metal poor" because they have far less than that amount. Population I stars have more of the heavier nuclei because, while both types of stars in their old age produce heavy nuclei by the nuclear processes going on inside them, population II stars begin with none of the heavy nuclei, while population I stars begin with ready-made heavy elements in the dust that is mixed with the gas from which they are formed.

## *THE EVOLUTION OF A STAR*

We see many different kinds of stars in the sky. Some are red and some are white; some are very bright giants and some are faint dwarfs. Some flash up in a great bright explosion while some are thought to be invisible black holes. Hidden in this bewildering variety of stars are clues to how stars are born, develop, and die. Some of the stars we see must be young stars, only recently formed. Some are mature stars, and some are stars that are already dying. If we could tell which stars are at what stage and looked at them in order of age, from the youngest to the

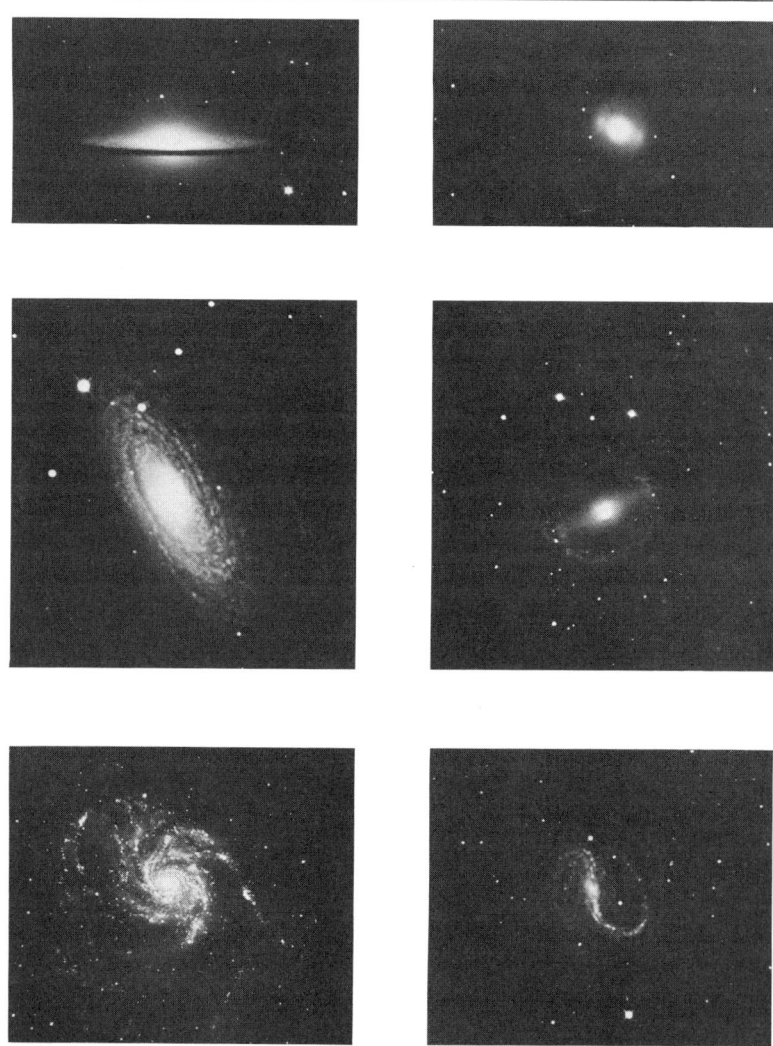

Six types of galaxies. Each one is an island universe like the Milky Way, made up of thousands of millions of stars.
HALE OBSERVATORIES

oldest, we would see the steps in the evolution of a star. Astronomers have found the clues and with their help have identified the stages in the development of a star.

One of the clues is the mass-luminosity curve, illustrated in Chapter 7, that shows that the more mass a star has, the brighter it is. A bright star, because it is sending out so much energy, must be burning up its atomic fuel very fast. The more mass a star has, the faster it burns its fuel, and the faster it grows old. Another clue came from studying the color-brightness chart for moving clusters of stars. Stars in a moving cluster must have been born together and must have the same chemical composition. Whatever differences there are among them must be due to differences in mass. But the more massive of them are the ones that grow old first. So the color-brightness charts of moving clusters help to identify which stars are young, which are mature, and which are advancing into old age. Other clues came from laboratory experiments that showed what temperature is needed for a particular nuclear process to begin, what raw materials are needed to feed the process, and what products come out of it.

The model of star development constructed from these and other clues shows that there are four stages in the evolution of a star: the formation stage, the main-sequence stage, the red-giant stage, and the dwarf stage. A star's condition at any moment can be represented by a point on the color-brightness chart. As the star evolves, that point moves on the chart.

THE FORMATION STAGE. A cloud of gas in space begins to contract as its atoms are drawn toward each other by the force of gravity. As it contracts, it begins to grow warmer. At first it radiates only infrared rays. Then, as the temperature increases, it becomes an orange-red star. When the temperature at the center of the star reaches about 10 million degrees Kelvin, a process of nuclear fusion begins in which hydrogen nuclei are combined to form helium nuclei. In this process, part of the mass is converted into energy, and the star, shining brightly, radiates the energy into space.

In the early days of this stage, when the star first begins to shine with orange-red light, the point that represents it on the color-brightness chart is on the right-hand side, since the star is red. It is low on the chart, since the star is faint to begin with. As the star brightens, the point rises, and as the color changes toward yellow and white, the point moves to the left, until it reaches the main sequence. It reaches the main sequence when nuclear fusion begins.

THE MAIN-SEQUENCE STAGE During this stage the star is fusing hydrogen to form helium. The fusion takes place only in the core of the star, where the temperature is high enough. In the outer, cooler layers of the star the hydrogen remains unchanged. As the fusion progresses, there is more and more helium in the core and less and less hydrogen.

THE RED-GIANT STAGE When all the hydrogen in the core is used up, the fusion of hydrogen stops for lack of fuel. The core then consists only of helium. While the fusion of hydrogen was going on, the energy it produced prevented the core from contracting under the force of gravity. When the fusion stops, the core contracts, and its temperature increases until it is high enough, about 100 million degrees Kelvin, for helium nuclei to fuse to form heavier elements. Again the core begins to release energy. The increase in temperature warms up the shell of hydrogen that surrounds the core and makes it expand. The star grows larger, and as its surface increases, so does its brightness. The star becomes a red giant. During its red-giant phase, the energy of the star comes from the fusion of helium in

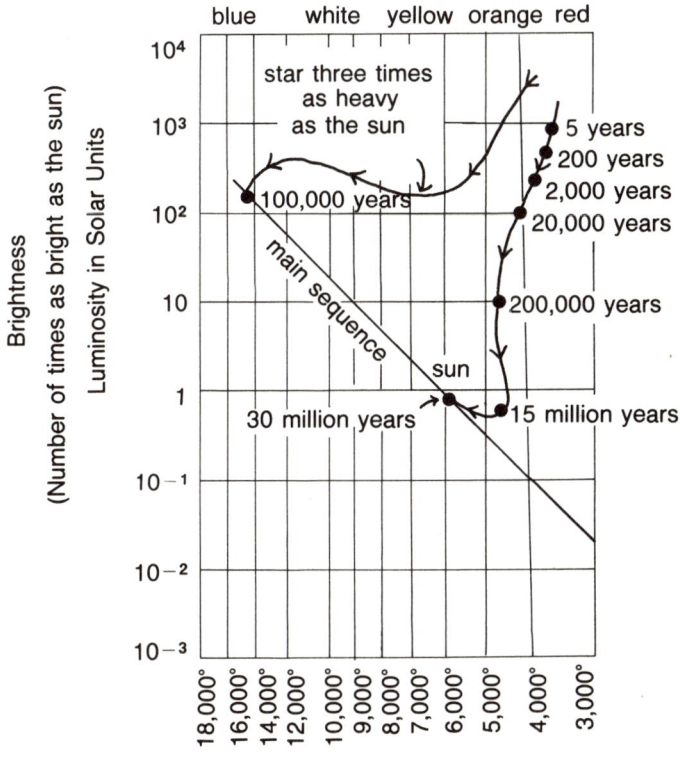

Evolution of a population I star: youth, from birth to the main sequence

its core. During the period when the star is becoming a red giant, the point that represents it on the color-brightness chart rises from the main-sequence line and moves to the right.

EXPLOSION AND THE DWARF STAGE When the helium in the core of the star is all used up, the energy that opposed the pull of gravity is again turned off. The star suddenly collapses. The sudden release of energy that results from the collapse makes the star explode and throw out masses of gas. A small star explodes as a nova, and what is left of it becomes a white dwarf. A massive star explodes as a supernova, and what is left of it becomes a neutron star. The heaviest neutron stars may be dense enough to become black holes.

During the main-sequence stage of the life of a star, there is more than one process that may take place to fuse hydrogen into helium. If the star's mass is less than one and a half times that of the sun, the process that produces helium is called the *proton-proton* process. In heavier stars, the temperature of the core goes above 20 million degrees Kelvin, which is high enough to start the *carbon cycle,* a more efficient process in which carbon, originally formed from helium, speeds up the process of fusing more helium nuclei.

The speed with which a star evolves depends on its mass. A star as massive as the sun makes the transition from formation to becoming a main-sequence star in 30 million years. A star three times as massive makes the transition in only one hundred thousand years. A star with the mass of the sun goes from birth to the red-giant stage in 1,000,000 million years. One three times as massive takes only 300 million years, while a star fifteen times as massive as the sun burns up so fast and furiously that it becomes a red giant in only 12 million years.

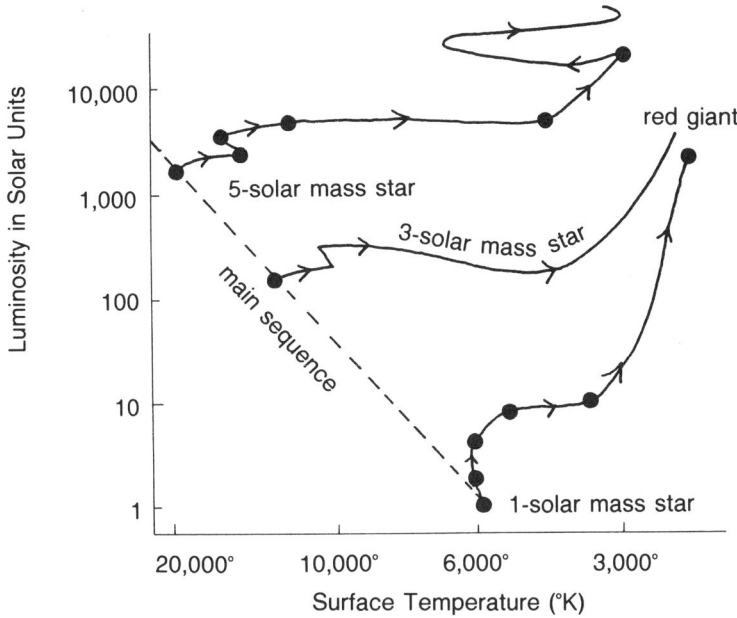

Evolution of a population I star: old age, from the main sequence to the red-giant stage

## THE CASE OF THE MISSING MASS

Will the universe ever stop expanding? The theoretical model of the expanding universe does not answer this question, but it tells astronomers where to look for the answer. The model shows that the universe will stop expanding and will begin to contract if the speed with which galaxies are moving apart slows down enough with the passage of time, and if the density of matter in the universe is great enough. Astronomers have made the appropriate measurements, and they give contradictory answers to the question.

To find out if the speed of the galaxies is slowing down, it is necessary to compare the speed they have now with the speed they had at different times in the past. This can be done because looking at distant galaxies is like looking into the past. If a galaxy is a thousand light-years away from us, its light takes a thousand years to reach us. So what we see by the red shift in this light is the speed away from us that the galaxy had one thousand years ago. But if the galaxy is a million light-years away, we see the speed it had a million years ago. A comparison of the red shifts of the most distant galaxies with those of the nearer ones seems to show that the galaxies have been slowing down enough for the expansion of the universe to stop at some future time.

The model of an expanding universe shows that the expansion will stop only if the density of matter in the universe is greater than a certain amount that has been calculated. Astronomers have compared with this amount the actual density of observed matter, calculated by adding up the estimated masses of all observed galaxies and the estimated mass of gas and dust in space and then dividing by the volume of the space in which these masses are spread out. The density turns out to be about one tenth as much as is needed to stop the expansion of the universe. If the measures of the slowing down of the rate of expansion are correct, then 90 percent of the mass of the universe is missing. Where is the missing mass? Is it hidden

# THE EVOLUTION OF THE STARS ☆ 141

A section of the Rosette Nebula in Monoceros HALE OBSERVATORIES

in black holes, which are invisible? This is a question that has not yet been answered.

## PEOPLE AND THE STARS

Compared to the universe, the earth is only a tiny speck of dust. We are imprisoned on it by its force of gravity and our need for food, warmth, and air. But we have dared to reach out into space. We have explored it with telescopes. Our spaceships have taken us to the moon, and rockets have traveled to Mars, Venus, and Jupiter.

Our ideas about the stars have been changed by our increasing knowledge. We used to think that the stars were faint lights on a sphere that turned around the earth. Now we know that they are bright suns scattered through space. We used to think the earth was the center of the universe. Now we know it is only a small companion of one of the smaller suns in a galaxy that is one of millions of galaxies. We have made mistakes, and we have found the means of correcting them. There are still many things about the stars that we do not know or understand. What caused the Big Bang? Why are there so many double stars? How far does the universe reach? Will its expansion ever stop? As we reach out into space with larger telescopes, and dig into the atom in laboratories, we will learn the answers to some of these questions.

# *Glossary*

ABERRATION OF LIGHT The shift in the direction from which starlight seems to come that is caused by the earth's motion around the sun.

ABSOLUTE MAGNITUDE The magnitude a star would have if it were ten parsecs away.

ANGSTROM The unit used to measure wavelengths of light. There are about ten million angstroms in a quarter of an inch.

BINARY STAR A double star, a star that may look like one star to the naked eye but is seen by other means to be two stars that are revolving around each other.

BLACK HOLE A small, very dense neutron star whose gravitational pull is so strong that no light can escape from it.

CENTRIFUGAL FORCE The force pushing away from the center when a body spins.

CEPHEID VARIABLE A throbbing star whose brightness changes, like the brightness of Delta Cephei.

COLOR INDEX The difference between the photographic magnitude and the visual magnitude of a star.

DENSITY OF A GAS The mass of one cubic unit of the gas.

DOPPLER EFFECT The lengthening (shift toward the red end) or shortening (shift toward the violet end) of the wavelengths in a star's spectrum, caused by the motion of the star away from or toward the observer.

DWARF STAR A very faint star. If it is white, the point that represents it on the color-brightness chart lies below the main sequence.

ECLIPSING BINARY A double star in which, as each member of the pair moves around the other, one passes between the earth and the other, temporarily cutting off some or all of its light.

FREQUENCY The number of vibrations per second, as in light of a given color.

GALAXY (with a capital *G*) The Milky Way, the pinwheel-shaped family of over 100,000 million stars to which the sun belongs.

GALAXY (with a small *g*) A great family of stars like the Galaxy and located outside the Galaxy.

GIANT STAR A very bright star. If it is red, the point that

represents it on the color-brightness chart lies above the main sequence.

GLOBULAR CLUSTER A ball-shaped group of up to a million stars. There are about a hundred of them scattered through the Galaxy, and they form a halo around its center.

HEAT INDEX The difference between the visual magnitude and the radiometric magnitude of a star.

INFRARED RAYS Electromagnetic waves with a lower frequency than red light.

LIGHT-YEAR The distance that light travels in a year (traveling at a speed of 186,000 miles per second).

LUMINOSITY A star's real brightness, or the amount of light that it sends out per unit of time.

MAGNITUDE OF A STAR A number that indicates the apparent brightness of a star. A low number indicates a bright star. A high number indicates a faint star.

MAIN SEQUENCE The line along which most of the points cluster in the color-brightness chart, showing that, for most stars, the redder a star is, the fainter it is.

MASS-LUMINOSITY CURVE The line along which the points are found to cluster when a graph is drawn in which each point stands for a star, and its position in the graph shows the mass of the star and the brightness of the star as the coordinates of the point in the graph.

NEUTRINOS Small, electrically neutral particles released when protons combine to form a helium nucleus.

NEUTRONS The particles inside an atomic nucleus that have no electrical charge.

NEUTRON STAR A star that consists entirely of neutrons.

NOVA A star that suddenly flares up to about a thousand times its original brightness and then becomes faint again.

NUCLEUS OF AN ATOM The core of the atom. It consists of protons and neutrons held together by the nuclear force.

PARALLAX OF A STAR The half width of the elliptical path that a star seems to trace on the sky sphere once a year. It is a measure of the distance to the star.

PARSEC A unit of distance used to measure the distances of stars. It is the distance a star would have to be from the earth to have a parallax of one second of arc. A parsec is about 3¼ light-years.

PECULIAR MOTION The motion of a star past all the other stars.

PERIOD The time it takes to complete one cycle in any change or motion that consists of repetition of the same cycle over and over again.

PERIOD-LUMINOSITY CURVE The line along which the points

are found to cluster when a graph is drawn in which each point stands for a Cepheid variable, and its position in the graph shows the period of the star's blinking and its real brightness as the coordinates of the point in the graph.

PHOTOGRAPHIC MAGNITUDE The measure of a star's magnitude obtained from a photograph.

PHOTONS The particles of energy in a stream of electromagnetic radiation. The amount of energy in each particle depends on the vibration frequency of the radiation.

POSITRONS Particles which are like electrons except that they have a positive electrical charge.

PROPER MOTION A star's motion as seen from the sun.

PROTONS The particles inside an atomic nucleus that have a positive electrical charge.

RADIOMETRIC MAGNITUDE The measure of a star's magnitude obtained by measuring the heat delivered by the starlight.

REFRACTION The bending of the path of starlight by the air.

REVERSING LAYER The cooler layer of gas at the surface of the sun or a star responsible for the dark lines in its spectrum.

SPECTROSCOPIC BINARY A double star recognized by the regular repetition of a Doppler shift of its spectrum alternately toward the red and violet ends.

SPECTRUM The arrangement, side by side, of the colors in light.

SUPERNOVA A star that suddenly flares up to about a million times its original brightness and then becomes faint again.

ULTRAVIOLET RAYS Electromagnetic waves with a higher frequency than violet light.

VISUAL BINARY A double star in which the two stars can be seen separately through a telescope.

VISUAL MAGNITUDE The measure of a star's magnitude as observed by eye.

WAVELENGTH OF LIGHT The distance that light of a fixed frequency travels in the time that it takes to make one vibration.

# Bibliography

Berendzen, Richard; Hart, Richard; and Seeley, Daniel. *Man Discovers the Galaxies.* New York: Science History Publications, 1976.

Motz, Lloyd. *The Universe: Its Beginning and End.* New York: Charles Scribner's Sons, 1976.

Pasachoff, Jay M. *Contemporary Astronomy.* Philadelphia: W. B. Saunders Company, 1977.

Shapley, Harlow, ed. *Source Book in Astronomy, 1900–1950.* Cambridge: Harvard University Press, 1960.

Shapley, Harlow, and Howarth, Helen E., eds. *A Source Book in Astronomy.* New York: McGraw-Hill, 1929.

Weinberg, Steven. *The First Three Minutes: A Modern View of the Origin of the Universe.* New York: Basic Books, 1977.

# Index

Aberration of light, 50–51
*Albireo,* 22, 64
*Aldebaran,* 24, 36
*Algol,* 20
*Alnitam (Alnilam),* 24
*Alpha Centauri,* 36
*Altair,* 22
*Andromeda,* 17–19
Angstrom, 31
*Antares,* 4, 23, 64, 96, 103, 108, 110
*Aquila,* 22
*Arcturus,* 22, 96, 103
Atomic nucleus, 112
*Auriga,* 25

*Betelgeuse,* 24–25
*Big Dipper,* 14–16, 22, 27, 64
Binaries, 64, 66, 71, 80–81
   eclipsing, 68–69
   spectroscopic, 68
   visual, 68, 81, 83
Black holes, 125, 138, 141
*Boötes,* 22
Brightness, 7, 35–45, 70, 93, 104
   apparent, 38–40, 44, 85, 91–92, 94, 101
   real, 39, 44–45, 83–85, 90–92, 94, 96–98, 101, 105–7, 117
   scale, 35–36, 43

*Canis Majoris,* 24
*Canis Minoris,* 24
*Canopus,* 36
*Capella,* 25, 96, 103
*Cassiopeia,* 14–15, 17–18, 20

Celestial north pole, 10–11, 14–15
Celestial south pole, 10–11
*Centaurus,* 43, 64
Cepheid variable, 70, 91–95, 100
*Cepheus,* 17–20
Chemical elements, 28, 112, 115
Clouds of dust and gas, 119
Color, 7, 102, 104–5, 107–8
Color-brightness chart, 96–97, 101, 135–139
Color index, 37, 102–3
*Crab Nebula,* 72
*Cygnus,* 21, 64

*Delta Cephei,* 19, 69
*Deneb,* 22, 44
Density, 109, 140
Deuterium, 122, 124
Direction, 7, 25–26, 40–42, 49, 52–55, 60, 65, 82, 87, 127
Distance, 35–45, 55, 86–101, 104, 127
Doppler effect, 58, 68, 88, 115, 121
*Draco,* 16, 18, 21, 27, 36
*Dubhe,* 15, 27
Dust, 74, 97–100, 104–5, 126, 132–33

Earth satellites, 112, 114, 122
Earth's orbit, 41
Electrons, 115, 120, 130
Elementary particles, 129
*Etamin,* 21, 27, 36
Evolution of stars, 128–142
Explosion and dwarf stage, 138

INDEX ☆ 151

Fixed stars, 3, 46
Formation stage, 135
Frequency of light, 30
Fuel of a star, 118, 135

Galaxies, 77–78, 99, 101, 114, 119, 124–25, 127, 129–30, 132, 139, 142
 exploding, 120
 spiral, 133
Gamma rays, 114, 126, 130
Gamma-ray window, 126
Gas clouds, 117
Giants, 97–98
Globular clusters, 76, 100, 125, 130, 132
Gravitation, 80–81, 84, 125, 131, 135–36, 141
*Great Nebula in Andromeda,* 18, 76, 98–99

Heat index, 37, 103
Helium, 33–34, 117–18, 127, 130, 133, 136, 138
*Hyades,* 24, 62, 64, 89
Hydrogen, 32, 117–18, 124, 127, 130, 136

Image intensifier, 112
Infrared rays, 30, 37, 114, 123–25, 135
Infrared window, 125
Interferometer, 109

*Kids,* the, 25

Light, definition of, 30
Light detectors, 112
Light waves, 114
Light-years, 42–43
*Little Dipper,* 15–16
Luminosity, 39
*Lyra,* 21, 27, 36, 61

*Magellanic Clouds,* 76, 91, 93–95
Magnitude, 35–36
 absolute, 44
 apparent, 40
 photographic, 37
 radiometric, 37
 visual, 37
Main sequence, 97, 109, 136, 138
Main-sequence stage, 136, 138
Mass, 81–85, 90, 104, 117, 135, 138
Mass-luminosity curve, 83–85, 89–90, 117, 135
*Merak,* 15, 27
Milky Way, 20–22, 74–76, 100, 104, 124
Missing mass, 139–42
Motion of a star, 46–61
 peculiar, 47, 51, 60–61
 proper, 51–55, 62, 65, 88–89
 space, 54, 59–60, 87
Motion of the sun, 60–61
Moving clusters, 62, 64, 86, 90, 135

Nearest star, 5–6, 43
Nebula, 76
Neutrinos, 127, 130
Neutrons, 116, 120, 130
Neutron star, 108–10, 120, 125, 138
*Northern Cross,* 21–22, 64
Nova, 71, 101, 138
Nuclear fusion, 136–37

OAO-II, 123–24
Observatories, flying, 114, 122
Orbits, 89
*Orion,* 23–24, 64, 74, 96
OSO, 123, 125

Parallax, 40–41, 43–44, 49–50, 81, 85–87, 90
Parsecs, 42–43
Particle detectors, 112
*Pegasus,* 18

## 152 ☆ INDEX

Period, 70, 81–82, 89, 94–95
Period-luminosity curve, 93, 95, 99–100
*Perseus,* 17–20, 64, 74
Photons, 114, 129
*Pleiades,* 18, 24, 64
Pointers, 15, 27
*Polaris,* 4, 15–16, 25
Population I, 99–100, 133
Population II, 100, 132–33
*Procyon,* 24
Proton, 116, 120, 129–30
*Proxima,* 43
Pulsar, 120, 125

Quasars, 124–25

Radiation, 114, 129
Radio astronomy, 6, 74, 114, 117–19, 121, 124–26
Red dwarf, 120
Red giant, 71, 99, 107–10, 137–39
Red-giant stage, 136
Red shift, 58, 67, 69–70, 78, 140
Refraction, 49
Reversing layer, 33
*Rigel,* 24, 44
Rockets, 112, 114, 141

*Sagittarius,* 23, 74
*Scorpius,* 22, 64
*Sirius,* 3–4, 24–25, 36, 39, 44, 64–65, 82–83, 96, 103, 109
 companion of, 108
Size, 104, 106
Sky sphere, 3–4, 9, 14, 25–27, 48, 51–53, 65, 82, 142
*Southern Cross,* 64
Spaceship, 112–13, 141

Spectral class, 95, 97–98, 100–101
Spectroscope, 121
Spectrum, 7–8, 29, 58, 77
 bright-line, 29, 34
 continuous, 29
 dark-line, 32–34, 39, 59, 67, 69–70, 72, 88, 95, 100, 103, 105, 115
Speed of light, 31
Spiral arms, 74, 99–100, 119, 133
Summer stars, 13, 21–22
Supernova, 72, 104, 138
Synchrotron radiation, 120

*Taurus,* 24, 36, 62
Temperature, 5, 37, 102–6, 115, 120, 129, 135–36

UHURU, 123, 125
Ultraviolet rays, 6, 30, 114, 117, 123–24
Ultraviolet window, 123
Universe, expanding, 121, 129, 139, 142

Van Maanen's star, 108
*Vega,* 21, 27, 31, 36, 61, 96
Violet shift, 58, 67, 69–70, 72

Wanderers, 3
Wavelength of light, 31
Weighing a star, 79–85
White dwarf, 71, 107–9, 138
Width, 106, 108–9, 117
Winter stars, 13, 23

X rays, 6, 114, 125
X-ray window, 125